3 3052 01662 0595

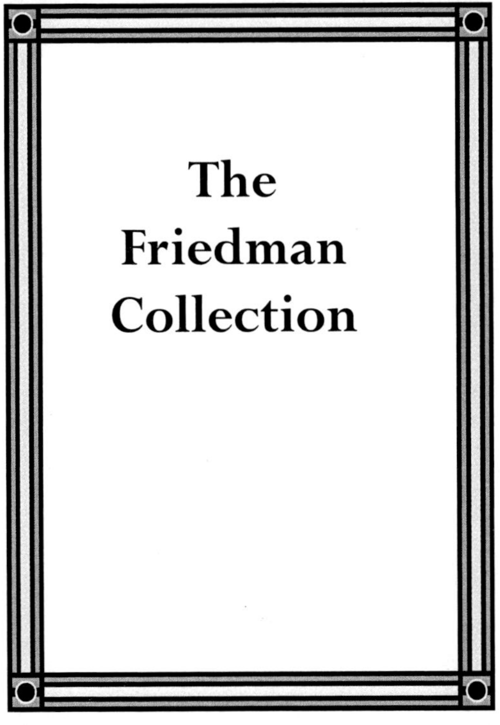

Praise for *SHRILL* by Lindy West

***NEW YORK TIMES* BESTSELLER**

ONE OF THE BEST BOOKS OF THE YEAR
NPR • *Esquire* • *Newsweek* • *Los Angeles Times*

"Read West's ferociously funny book and you'll be shouting her praises."
—*People*

"Stitch-inducing and searingly honest. . . . West takes readers through her journey from a self-effacing child working to keep her body and voice small to an unapologetic, fat-positive feminist, skewering the status quo one keyboard stroke at a time."
—*USA Today*

"Lindy West is the troll-fighting feminist warrior you've been waiting for. . . . *Shrill* treats feminism, fatness, and social change with rigorous attention without losing any of West's signature humor."
—*Los Angeles Times*

"[West is] one of the most distinctive voices advancing feminist politics through humor. . . . With patience, humor, and a wildly generous attitude toward her audience [West] meets readers at their point of prejudice so that she may, with little visible effort, shepherd them toward a more humane point of view."
—*The New York Times Book Review*

"[B]eautiful, joyful writing. . . . West defies clichés both by being persistently hilarious and deeply loving."
—*Washington Post*

"Hilarious, biting, and wise."
—Huffington Post

"Lindy West's memoir is a witty and cathartic take on toxic misogyny and fat shaming. She comes to accept her body just as Internet trolls congregate en masse to try to rip this new confidence from her, but she's rearing to fight back. . . . In *Shrill*, West is our fat, ferocious, and funny avenging angel."
—NPR, Best Books of 2016

"Reading West's book is like taking a master class in inclusivity and cultural criticism, as taught by one of the funniest feminists alive today." —Refinery29

"An emotional roller coaster. One moment you're snorting from laughter, trying to avoid all the weird looks you're getting on the train. The next you're silently absorbing a larger truth neatly packaged into the perfect sentence you didn't expect to read."

—*Mother Jones*

"With her clear-eyed insights into modern culture and her confidence in her own intelligence and personal worth, West appeals to the humanity of even the most parents' basement-dwelling, misogynistic, and casually hateful of trolls."

—*Esquire*, Best Books of 2016

"[West's] writing is sharp, smart, hilarious, relatable, insightful, and memorable. She tackles serious and personal subjects—like being fat, getting an abortion, feeling lonely, or dealing with harassment online—and is just as capable of eliciting tears as laughter . . . I dare you to pick up a copy." —*Newsweek*, Best Books of 2016

"It's hard to discuss SHRILL without being effusive. It's hard to write about it without offering gratitude, and pullquotes such as 'this is the best and most important book I've read all year.' But it's certainly no exaggeration to say we're all very lucky to live in a world where Lindy West exists. . . . When she writes 'I hope I helped,' you want to enthusiastically respond, 'more than you can ever know.'"

—*The Globe and Mail* (Toronto)

"Poignant, hilarious, and contemplative." —*Cosmopolitan*

"One of the most impressive aspects of this book is the level of nuance, self-reflection, and humanity that West displays in her analysis of her own writing and her relationships with others. . . . It's the best kind of memoir, and it shows that Lindy West still has a lot more to say—and that we should all keep listening." —Bitch Media

"West is utterly candid and totally hilarious . . . as funny as she is incisive." —*Vogue*

"With *Shrill*, West cements her reputation as a woman unafraid to comfort (and confound) her critics. . . . [*Shrill*] illustrates just how deeply sexism pervades our society while laughing at the absurdities that sexism somehow normalizes." —*Elle*

"Lindy West can take almost any topic and write about it in a way that is smart, funny, warm, and unique." —Bustle

"West is candid and funny, unafraid to criticize rape jokes or explain how airlines discriminate against fat people, and her fearlessness has made her one of the most notable voices on the Internet." —Flavorwire

"Both sharp-toothed and fluid. . . . West is propulsively entertaining." —Slate

"Lindy West did not set out to be a feminist warrior against the forces that wish to silence and hurt women for doing things that men take for granted. . . . *Someone* has to fight the misogynists, after all, and West is well-situated for the front lines, lacing her blunt sense of humor with a surprising amount of nuanced empathy, even for those out there who are the ugliest to women." —Salon

"Lindy West is one of the Great Ladies of the Feminist Internet. . . . 250 pages of pure hilariousness." —Feministing

"Incredible and insightful. . . . What West ultimately strives for is to incrementally make those small changes that can lead to something so much bigger and better for us all." —Amy Poehler's Smart Girls

"[West is] warm and cutting, vulnerable and funny in equal measures; her sense of self makes you yourself feel seen." —BuzzFeed

"Hey reader! I thought I'd read enough in this lifetime about people's childhoods and feelings and such and I'd never want to do it again. But Lindy West is such a totally entertaining and original writer she kind of blew that thought out of my head halfway into the first chapter. I dare you to feel differently."

—Ira Glass, *This American Life*

"You have to be careful about what you read when you're writing, or you can end up in total despair, thinking, 'This is what I wanted to say, only she got there first and said it better.'"

—Jennifer Weiner, number one New York Times bestselling author of *Good in Bed* and *The Littlest Bigfoot*

"The surge of love and joy I felt while crylaughing through this book almost made my cold dead heart explode. Lindy is so smart and so funny that it almost hurts my little jealous-ass feelings. She is my most favorite writer ever."

—Samantha Irby, author of *Meaty: Essays*

"It made me hurt, both from laughing and crying. Required reading if you are a feminist. Recommended reading if you aren't."

—Jenny Lawson, number one bestselling author of *Let's Pretend This Never Happened (A Mostly True Memoir)* and *Furiously Happy: A Funny Book About Horrible Things*

"It's literally the new *Bible*."

—Caitlin Moran, best-selling author of *How to Be a Woman*

"There's a reason Lindy West is such a beloved writer: she gets to the heart of impossible issues with humor and grace. West will have you cringing, laughing, and crying, all within one page. *Shrill* is a must-read for all women."

—Jessica Valenti, author of *Why Have Kids?: A New Mom Explores the Truth About Parenting and Happiness* and *Full Frontal Feminism: A Young Woman's Guide to Why Feminism Matters*

The Witches Are Coming

Also by LINDY WEST

Shrill: Notes from A Loud Woman

The Witches Are Coming

Lindy West

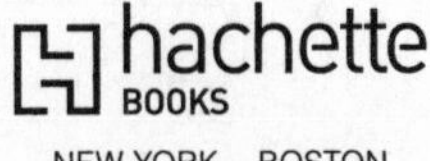

NEW YORK BOSTON

Copyright © 2019 by Lindy West

Cover design by Amanda Kain
Cover copyright © 2019 by Hachette Book Group, Inc.

Portions of this book were previously published in different form in the *New York Times*, the *Guardian*, and Jezebel.

Hachette Book Group supports the right to free expression and the value of copyright. The purpose of copyright is to encourage writers and artists to produce the creative works that enrich our culture.

The scanning, uploading, and distribution of this book without permission is a theft of the author's intellectual property. If you would like permission to use material from the book (other than for review purposes), please contact permissions@hbgusa.com. Thank you for your support of the author's rights.

Hachette Books
Hachette Book Group
1290 Avenue of the Americas
New York, NY 10104
hachettebookgroup.com
twitter.com/hachettebooks

First Edition: November 2019

Hachette Books is a division of Hachette Book Group, Inc.
The Hachette Books name and logo are trademarks of Hachette Book Group, Inc.

The publisher is not responsible for websites (or their content) that are not owned by the publisher.

The Hachette Speakers Bureau provides a wide range of authors for speaking events. To find out more, go to www.hachettespeakersbureau.com or call (866) 376-6591.

Print book interior design by Timothy Shaner, NightandDayDesign.biz

Library of Congress Cataloging-in-Publication Data has been applied for.

ISBNs: 9780316449885 (hardcover); 9780316534918 (signed edition); 9780316534925 (B&N signed edition); 9780306873492 (B&N Black Friday signed edition); 9780316449892 (ebook); 9780316449878 (library book)

Printed in the United States of America

LSC-C

10 9 8 7 6 5 4 3 2 1

To the kids.

Trust your instincts.
Believe your eyes.

CONTENTS

Introduction: They Let You Do It 1
Choosing the Lie 21
Is Adam Sandler Funny? 38
Ted Bundy Was Not Charming—Are You High*?* 52
How to Be a Girl 65
Always Meet Your Heroes 76
Do, Make, Be, Barf 91
A Giant Douche Is a Good Thing if You're a Giant . . 107
Gear Swap 122
Joan 141
Obsolescence Is a Preventable Disease 154
What Is an Abortion, Anyway? 165
Leave Hell to the Devils 180
Anger Is a Weapon 199
Magic Isn't Magic 209
The World Is Good and Worth Fighting For 219
Long Live the Port Chester Whooping Cranes 233
Tomorrow Is the First Day 253
Acknowledgments 260

Introduction: They Let You Do It

Not long ago, my husband was at a bar in Chicago. A friend had told him to check out this particular bar because it's a cool dive run by queer people of color, with dancing and cheap drinks and a good vibe. So he was sitting there, having a beer, and after a while a guy came in and sat down next to him. White guy, late forties. Polo shirt. Mustache probably. Khaki shorts. Standard random white guy.

The guy—his name was Larry or Barry or something, so for the purposes of this story let's call him LarryBarry—struck up a conversation with my husband, asked him if he was having fun. My husband said, "Yeah, this is a fun bar! People are dancing. It's cool." And the guy got a real sad look on his face and said, "Yeah, this is one of my favorite songs. I wish I was dancing right now." So naturally my husband asked, "Well, why don't you go dance?"

And LarryBarry said, "I'M NOT ALLOWED TO DANCE."

My husband was confused. There did not seem to be any posted restrictions on who was or was not allowed to dance. Other people were dancing. So he inquired, "Larry-Barry, why are you not allowed to dance?"

And then LarryBarry told his tale:

"Well, two nights ago, I came to this bar, because it's the closest bar to my house, and I come here all the time. And they were having a dance night, and I love to dance. So I went out on the dance floor, and there were some people out there dancing, so I just started dancing with this girl, and she said, 'I don't really want to dance with you,' and then her friend got all weird about it. So now I guess I'm *not allowed to dance*."

Can you believe that? He's not allowed to dance!

This is what it's come to, ladies and gentlemen. This is what the PC police have done to us. It's as though the PC police don't even care how much LarryBarry likes that song! Or how important it is that he continue his ongoing research into the worst ways to move the human body!

Well, sorry if I don't want to live in a world where straight white men in their forties with mustaches can't go to the queer POC dance night and nonconsensually grind on lesbians they don't know without people getting weird about it! Last time I checked, this was America!

My husband said kindly, "LarryBarry, I'm pretty sure if you just go out there and dance and don't touch anyone, you'll be fine."

And LarryBarry thought, "Hmm, don't touch anyone? What's that?" But he decided to go for it, and as he got up from the bar he looked my husband in the eyes and said, man to man, "If something goes wrong out there, will you back me up?"

And my husband said, "If something goes wrong, you will look over here, and you will find that this chair is empty, and you will never see me again, because I don't know you."

This modern fable—the Ballad of LarryBarry—tells us quite a bit about our current moment in history.

It seems that a lot of men are confusing being asked not to violate other people's sexual boundaries with being forbidden to participate in basic human activities such as dancing, dating, chatting, walking around, going to work, and telling jokes.

One thing we've been hearing a lot recently when a man—particularly a man a lot of people really like—is accused of something awful is that the accusations aren't real but in fact are part of a baseless, bloodthirsty, politically motivated mass hysteria known as a "witch hunt."

This is a relatively new usage of the term. Traditionally, "witch hunt" has been used in reference to the witch trials of early modern Europe and colonial America, during which an estimated 40,000 to 60,000 people were brutally tortured by being briefly ostracized at work and having a lot of people yell at them.

Wait. That's wrong. They were actually hanged, beheaded, or burned at the stake. Still, though. Very, very similar to the modern-day witch hunts against rapists!

Imagine, if you will, a fine woodcut print of a colonial witch burning. A town square, a black sky, perhaps a fat bristly pig. A massive bonfire crackles hungrily, and at its heart, three screaming women are bound to a post, burning to death in agony. Nearby, a group of angry men in pantaloons and buckled hats stoke the flames with long poles. A bat-winged demon harries the dying women from above, while all around the townspeople froth at the mouth and howl in a frenzy of bloodlust. Here and there, corpses litter the ground, but the townspeople seem not to notice or care. Some fricking knave beheads the pig with a sword.

Now, in case you're not familiar with classic seventeenth-century iconography, I, an art historian,* have compiled a handy reference guide to what each of these elements represents:

Women burning to death = Men who did nothing wrong

* Honorary degree, Trump University.

Men stoking the fire = Feminists (third-wave, booooooooo!)
Demon = How Sharon's butt looked in those pants
The fire = Call-out culture
Townspeople = The court of public opinion
The pig = Due process
The knave = Salma Hayek
Corpses = Free speech, comedy, human reproduction, the legacy of Matt Lauer

I think we can all agree that this fully checks out and that, indeed, it is men who are the true victims of witch hunts. Which they invented. To kill women.

But the "witch hunt" deflection isn't only for rapes! It has the power to transform pretty much any credible accusation against a man into an unfair—nay, unconstitutional—and unfounded smear campaign. Accused of racism? Witch hunt! Accused of undermining the integrety of democracy itself? Witch hunt! Accused of willfully letting children die in concentration camps on the southern border of the United States? A pure, unadulterated, hysterical, bitchy witch hunt!!!

Perhaps no one is as fond of this rhetorical maneuver as the United States' forty-fifth president, Donald J. Trump. Based on a simple Twitter search, he has tweeted the phrase at least two hundred times since taking office, betraying a ceaseless, all-consuming paranoid panic that is definitely safe and good to have in a world leader. A minuscule sampling of the fucking hundreds of them I found:

> May 15, 2016: "The media is really on a witch-hunt against me. False reporting, and plenty of it - but we will prevail!"
> January 10, 2017: "FAKE NEWS - A TOTAL POLITICAL WITCH HUNT!"
> February 27, 2018: "WITCH HUNT!"
> March 19, 2018: "A total WITCH HUNT with massive conflicts of interest!"
> April 10, 2018: "A TOTAL WITCH HUNT!!!"
> April 22, 2018: "A complete Witch Hunt!"
> May 23, 2018: "WITCH HUNT!"
> June 5, 2018: " . . . The greatest Witch Hunt in political history!"
> August 22, 2018: "NO COLLUSION - RIGGED WITCH HUNT!"
> December 13, 2018: "WITCH HUNT!"
> January 26, 2019: "WITCH HUNT!"

Very normal, very cool!

So, just to clarify, you guys get to be the witch-hunters *and* the witches *and* the witch-hunter-hunters who hunt down any witches who are witch-hunting too hard. And the rest of us get burned.

To be fair, Donald Trump framing himself as a witch actually makes a bit more sense than it does for most of the guilty little wormies who try to do it. Every iota of Trump's success is a con, a dark magic trick, built on illusion and hypnosis and the impenetrable magical thinking of his followers. Even the repetition in those tweets—WITCH HUNT, WITCH HUNT, WITCH HUNT—is a kind of incantation, calling itself into being. *Of course* a man whose only skill is putting his name on shit understands the power of branding.

Trump is not a witch, but he is adept at one spell. He knows that, at least in this country at the moment, all you have to do is say something is true. If you say you're a self-made billionaire, you're a billionaire. If you say you'll make something great, sure, it will be. It's a witch hunt? If you say so.

Let's go back to before the fullest expression of the power of that brand. It was October 2016, and we were doing so well. It felt like we were doing so well, anyway. Thanks to decades of bloody, incremental, hard-won victories by generations of activists and organizers, the traditional presumption of white male authority had grown translucent, vulnerable. The term *feminist* was no longer so stigmatized that teenage girls were afraid to assert their innate equality and celebrities were afraid to utter it in interviews. Marriage equality passed, and the pits of Hell did not open beneath us. Black Lives Matter forced the facts of racialized police violence through the generally impenetrable psyches of Middle Americans, whether they liked it or not. Sure, the environment was fucked and we'd been at war for nearly twenty years (since I was a teenager and since my teenagers were babies), but there was a palpable momentum, an undeniable feeling that progress had the upper hand. We were just a hairsbreadth from electing the United States' first female president to succeed the United States' first black president. Justice Antonin Scalia passed away unexpectedly and, despite Mitch McConnell's best efforts at subverting democracy, *she* was going to choose his replacement. We weren't done, but we were doing it.

And then, true to form—like the Balrog's whip catching Gandalf by his little gray bootie, like the husband in a Lifetime movie hissing "If I can't have you, no one can"—white American voters and the electoral college and a few Russian troll farms shoved an incompetent, racist con man into the White House.

Trump wasn't a former reality TV star, a failed businessman who became an actor who played a successful businessman on a bad TV show—he was a *current* reality TV star. He came straight from the set. And to regurgitate the first and most basic President Trump media take, he brought not just his showbiz sensibilities but his *reality TV instincts* into the Oval Office: a savant's understanding of Americans' hunger for "reality" over reality, for the outrageous, for the cruelty of Simon Cowell and the brazen individualism of "I'm not here to make friends."

Reality TV, as we all know by now, is scripted. This is the most frightening vestige of President Trump's TV career: in his world, reality doesn't dictate the script; the script dictates reality. When reality doesn't favor or flatter him, he simply says what he *wants* to be true. And in the minds of his fanatics—absolutely blitzed on a decade or three of antimedia, antiacademia, paranoiac propaganda—it *becomes true*. It's a kind of magic.

A vast and verdant journalistic subgenre has sprung up around the president's passion for lying: websites devoted solely to fact checking, ever-lengthening lists of falsehoods at major media outlets. The *Washington Post*'s Fact Checker page reported (at the time of this writing) that Trump had made 10,796 false or misleading statements during the first 869 days of his presidency. After special counsel Robert Mueller released his report on Russian interference in the 2016 election in April 2019, Trump tweeted, "No collusion. No obstruction. For the haters and the radical left Democrats—GAME OVER," never mind the fact that the report said no such thing. Thanks to the baby-soft Left's willingness to hear all "sides" of an "argument," no matter how blatantly disingenuous, even Trump's most obvious rewritings of reality, from the relatively benign (the size of his inauguration crowd) to the truly dangerous (the "very fine people" marching for white supremacy in Charlottesville), have been entered into the public record with some degree of legitimacy. Even people who didn't overtly hate Hillary Clinton took "Lock her up!" to the polls with them, and maybe just enough of them had just enough doubt that they skipped over that bubble or didn't bother to go at all. Who knows what kind of an impact that tiny margin could have had, cumulatively, when replicated over a population of 245 million eligible voters?

The infamous *Access Hollywood* tape was the first time we really saw Donald Trump's plot armor in action. On the tape, which was recorded in 2005 and resurfaced just before the 2016 election, you can hear Billy Bush—a first cousin of the man we were *so sure* would be history's worst president—wheezing ecstatically as Trump brags, inadvertently into a hot mic, about sexually harassing and groping women. The pair, along with a passel of unidentified men, were on a bus en route to film an *Access Hollywood* segment with the actress Arianne Zucker.

Through the window of the bus, Bush seems to spot Zucker first, as she waits to greet them. "Sheesh," he blurts out, breathless, telling Trump how hot "your girl" is. You can feel Bush's giddiness, a contact high, at getting to join a more powerful man in the oldest and most sacred of male bonding exercises: objectifying women.

Trump spies Zucker too. "Whoa!"

"Yes!" Bush grunts, Beavis-esque. "Yes, the Donald has scored!"

Of course, "the Donald" has not "scored." The Donald is on the NBC lot to shoot a guest appearance on *Days of Our Lives* at the behest of his employer to promote his reality show, *The Apprentice*, while *Access Hollywood* produces an accompanying puff piece. This is work within work within work. Bush is at work. Trump is at work. Zucker is at work, and not only is she not Trump's "girl," she is a complete stranger who is also on camera and being paid to smile.

"Heh heh heh," Bush snickers. "My man!"

Such has it always been: powerful men sorting women's bodies into property and trash and "good" guys, average guys, guys you know, guys you love, guys on the *Today* show, going along with it. Snickering. Licking a boot here and there, joining in if they're feeling especially bitter or transgressive or insecure or far from the cameras that day. Perhaps, at their most noble, staying silent. Never speaking up, because the social cost is too high. It's easier to leave that for the victims to bear. After all, they're used to it.

"I gotta use some Tic Tacs," Trump says, still inside the bus, "just in case I start kissing her. You know, I'm automatically attracted to beautiful—I just start kissing them, it's like a magnet. Just kiss. I don't even wait. And when you're a star, they let you do it. You can do anything. Grab them by the pussy. You can do anything." Bush and the bus toadies laugh.

Every woman knows a version of Donald Trump. Most of us have known more of them than we can (or care to) recall. He's the boss who thinks you owe him something; the date who thinks that silence means "yes" and "no" means "try harder"; the stranger who thinks your body's mere existence constitutes an invitation to touch, take, own, and destroy. He's every deadbeat hookup, every narcissistic loser, every man who's ever tried to leverage power, money, fame, credibility, or physical strength to snap your boundaries like matchsticks. He is hot fear and cold dread and a pit in your stomach. He's the man who held you back, who never took you seriously, who treated you like nothing until you started to believe it, who raped you and told you it was your fault and whose daddy was a cop, so who would believe you anyway?

Donald Trump is rape culture's blathering id, and just a few days after the *Access Hollywood* tape dropped, then Democratic nominee Hillary Clinton (who, no doubt, has just as many man-made scars as the rest of us) was required to stand next to him on a stage for a presidential debate and remain unflappable while being held to an astronomically higher standard and pretend that he was her equal while his followers persisted in howling that sexism is a feminist myth. While Trump bragged about sexual assault and vowed to suppress disobedient media, cable news pundits spent their time taking a protractor to Clinton's smile—a constant, churning microanalysis of nothing, a subtle subversion of democracy that they are poised to repeat in 2020. And then she lost. (Actually, in a particularly painful living metaphor, she won, but because of institutional peculiarities put in place by long-dead white men, they took it from her and gave it to the man with fewer votes.)

In the intervening years, I have returned again and again to what Donald told Billy on the bus. "When you're a star they let you do it," he said. They let you do it. "It" being assault. "They" being a soap star unlucky enough to be standing near him or a businesswoman seated next to him on a flight or a reporter for *People* magazine on a tour of Mar-a-Lago or an aspiring model at a nightclub or a contestant on *The Apprentice* or Miss Finland 2006 or any of the other twenty-two (and counting) women who have accused the forty-fifth president of the United States of sexual assault, sexual harassment, and rape. Setting aside the fact that a touch or a sex act cannot be both consensual and non-consensual, how much can any population with little institutional power really be said to "let" themselves be victimized by the powerful? Systemic inequality makes choice an illusion.

"They let you do it" was in 2005. In 2017, Harvey Weinstein, the Hollywood mogul behind half of your favorite shit, everything from *Pulp Fiction* to *Project*

Runway, was exposed as a serial sexual predator. Dozens of women accused Weinstein of rape and sexual abuse, a pattern of coercive behavior that had lasted for at least three decades despite being an open secret in Hollywood and the press. Through some combination of time, rage, incremental political victories, and feminist sweat, we did not let him do it anymore.

(Weinstein also once, in 2016, told my husband to "keep it down" in a hotel bar, and my husband, not recognizing Weinstein, said, "Excuse me?" and Weinstein wilted like a tiny baby buttercup and was like "Oh, I guess, uh, we did sit a little bit close to you, sorry," and my husband said, "Yeah, you did," and Harvey Weinstein skulked away licking his own ass like a beaten dog, and this is my porno.)

As I'm sure you're aware if you're reading this book, the allegations against Weinstein—or, more accurately, the fact that an undeniable number of high-profile victims came forward and the allegations actually stuck—formed the keystone of a collective grassroots awakening known as the "Me Too" movement, started by the activist Tarana Burke in 2006. Since then, #MeToo has exploded into a large-scale cultural reckoning that so far has not remotely faded, victims striding bravely and angrily out of the shadows to tell their stories of exploitation, predation, terror, abuse, derailed careers, and sabotaged potential for the first time, as well as building bridges of solidarity across industries and socioeconomic strata to demand meaningful, widespread, systemic change.

Or, you might know it as *the thing where men get into trouble.*

Men have been very concerned about the thing where men get into trouble. Almost as soon as powerful men began falling to the truth (and by "falling" I mean "having to say sorry for bad things they chose to do and retreat to their mansions for a few months before booking sold-out comeback tours"), other men began *just asking questions* about redemption, about forgiveness, about when reckoning goes too far and turns into a witch hunt.

And look. I am sympathetic to people who feel they're being left behind in this new world. In a lot of ways, we all are. I understand that it's scary to suddenly face consequences for things that used to be socially acceptable—I grew up on Pepé Le Pew too—and I hear a lot of agita from men about how they're going to adapt. Won't it affect women's upward mobility if men are afraid to work with them? How are people supposed to date and procreate in this minefield? What if I get fired over a simple misunderstanding? If we believe victims unconditionally, won't the mob eventually come for us all?

I'm sorry to say it, but you just might have to tiptoe through the minefield for a while. We're tearing down old systems, but we haven't built new systems yet. (*Feeling uncomfortable at work? What's that like?*)

Let's return for a moment to LarryBarry, who wasn't allowed to dance. For the purposes of a cleaner narrative flow, I considered fudging the truth and telling you that it was me who had the encounter with LarryBarry at the bar, instead of relaying the story secondhand through my husband. It would have made for smoother storytelling.

But I realized that the story doesn't work with me sitting at the bar, because LarryBarry would never have said that to me. The frustration that LarryBarry expressed to my husband—at not being "allowed" to dance anymore because women are so sensitive these days—was contingent on the assumption of a shared understanding, a collective lamentation between men. He wasn't trying to complain to my husband; he was trying to commiserate with him—about the loss of power and freedom, of no longer being the one who makes the rules, of no longer having the benefit of the doubt in every interaction.

This moment in history is about more than individual interactions between individual people. Those matter, too—it matters how you made your subordinate feel with that comment, and it matters quite a lot that the woman on the bus went home and sobbed after you groped her—but, as Rebecca Traister wrote in December 2017 on The Cut: "This moment isn't just about sex. It's really about work."

It's about who feels at home in the workplace and who feels like an outsider—which, by extension, dictates who gets to thrive and ascend, who gets to hire their replacements, who gets to set their children up for success, who gets credit and glory, and who gets forgotten. It's about who feels safe in public spaces and who doesn't. Which is to say, it's about everything.

There's so much talk right now about being on the wrong side or the right side of history. The truth is that we have no idea whether the things we do are going to land us on the right side or the wrong side. Who knows how people are going to talk about meat eaters in two hundred years? There's a vegan lady who comes on my Instagram and calls me a rapist for drinking milk, and I hate that lady! But maybe she's right!

The reason #MeToo has been so terrifying to so many people is that we got a quick glimpse of what history is going to say about us. For just a moment, we could see the curvature of the earth.

We have a lot to figure out. The very foundations of our culture are marbled with violence, exploitation, and exclusion—the work of brilliant abusers (and mediocre ones), the institutional scaffolding that enabled them, and the invisible absence of their victims. Separating art from artist, to some degree, may not be a choice. We can't un-Michael-Jackson music or de-Alfred-Hitchcock film—nor, necessarily, should we. I don't know the answers. We also have to build mechanisms for navigating the uncomfortable fact that social movements predicated on believing victims are vulnerable to bad-faith exploitation. We have to be honest with ourselves about why Bill Cosby is the only high-profile #MeToo perpetrator who's seen a day in prison as of 2019. Accountability hurts, but what's the alternative? The way things were? Harvey Weinstein loosening his bathrobe while your daughter cowers in front of him?

Just like Trump, America loves to lie about itself, and Americans love to eat those lies up—anything that obliterates our sins, that tells us everything will be okay, that makes us the infallible, gallant protagonist in the story of Earth. We must root out the assumptions we swallow as fact and the facts we deny. We must not just examine but actively counter the disastrous, narcissistic death grip of mediocre white men on our past century's art, media, and politics. We must start telling true stories about who we are, who is free and who is not, what we are doing to the planet.

This moment feels destabilizing, hopeful but precarious, as though everything could change or nothing could change. We have flesh-and-bone evidence sitting in the White House—butt chugging Fox News and eating cheeseburgers and always disturbingly, profoundly alone—of exactly how far the status quo will go to protect itself. We know how deeply racial and gender hierarchies are built into the foundational myths of this country and by extension our stories, our pop culture, our darkest instincts, our most hidden conditioning. We know it's not just "locker room talk," no matter how many times Melania says so, and she knows it, too.

At the same time, have we ever been able to see it all more clearly? I cannot remember a more frightening time in all my life. And I cannot remember a time with more moral clarity.

If the Left's loathing of George W. Bush energized us to fight for and ultimately elect Barack Obama, what kind of political revolution might Trump engender? We can only see glimpses so far, but the momentum is real. A record 117 women were elected in the 2018 midterms. Democratic socialist Alexandria Ocasio-Cortez, twenty-nine, the youngest woman ever elected to Congress, has since been terrorizing the GOP with steely competence and actually knowing how to use Twitter. A historic number of female candidates have entered the race for the 2020 Democratic presidential nomination. Whatever the outcome of that election, we have now seen, for the first time in history, enough women together on a presidential debate stage that the fact of their gender cannot be central. It might be too late for me to think I could be president, but it is not too late for our daughters. And all the activists and organizers and storytellers and parents and politicians who've been doing this hard work for decades *without* solidarity, without acclaim—they're all still here, too. There are so, so many of us.

If there is magic in Trump's ability to conjure reality out of hot air and spittle, there is an equally powerful magic in the opposite: in speaking the truth, unvarnished, about what we see, what we remember, what has been done to us by people who have assumed power and status as a birthright, rules written just for them. People who are nervous or just trying to wait this moment out until everything settles down. There is power in saying, no, we will not settle down. We will not go back. It's the lifting of a veil, the opposite of a glamour. We have to be the witches they've always said we are, and counter their magic with our own.

So fine, if you insist. This is a witch hunt. We're witches, and we're hunting you.

Choosing the Lie

The first and best viral cat was Lil Bub. A brown tabby with sweet white paws, tiny from congenital dwarfism, tongue lolling between malformed jaws, Bub swept into our lives like a tsunami: low, slow, then deceptively swift, then inexorable, reshaping the land itself. One day we did not know there was a bowlegged, walleyed cat in Bloomington, Indiana; the next day the internet would never be the same.

The internet of 2011 was not quite the internet of now. Instagram had launched only a year prior, in October 2010, and—despite the success of early meme farms such as I Can Has Cheezburger? and the proliferation of cat videos on the young YouTube—viral content still had some spontaneity left in it, some guilelessness, some shades of outsider art. Users on Tumblr and Reddit, where Bub made her debut, posted photos of cute cats because they thought other users would like to see photos of cute cats, not to start a business. Social media wouldn't become terminally self-aware for another few years. In 2011, the notion that one could turn one's cat (or one's thigh gap or one's overnight oats or one's Kylie Jenner) into a brand, and turn that brand into a living, had not yet been born.

Into that relatively innocent media landscape waddled Lil Bub, and the internet lost its collective mind.

Bub's infirmity drew us to her as much as her cuteness; she was frail, our furry Beth March, with Beth's pure heart and unfortunate destiny to be the fulcrum for others' growth. We were doing Bub a favor by loving her, weren't we? Her face was ours to get over, to find cute in spite of itself, because we were so open-minded, so brave. But she was also just a cat, and that was our justification for fixing our gaze shamelessly on Bub's differentness.

In the most uncharitable reading of Lil Bub fever (a microcosm of the viral internet machine at large), we, her audience, do not come off well. We are ravenous, exploitative, selfish. You can ogle a cat. You can objectify a cat.

But then, Bub *is* cute, and she *is* a cat, and cats are not human beings, and it rarely does anyone any favors to draw equivalencies between real oppression and things that are not. So I don't know.

Maybe the only thing to do, when you are one speck in an ungovernable community of nearly eight billion people on this planet, is to always keep an eye trained on the deep *why* of things: Why do I like this? Where is this impulse coming from? Am I telling the truth to myself about myself?

People love to watch viral videos in which one kindly fisherman saves one sea turtle from a snarl of trash; they are less passionate about electing politicians who will dismantle policies that entrench corporate power and allow companies to pump poison into the oceans and skies in order to shore up the immoral wealth of billionaires and further destabilize the lives of the poor who will remain locked in toil until the planet boils us all to death as Jeff Bezos waves good-bye from his private rocket. Strange!

Bub is a benign example of our propensity to flatten our objets d'entertainment into mascots, trading cards, so we can consume them without the complications of flesh and blood and history (remember 2011's Homeless Man with the Golden Voice?), but that doesn't make the discussion irrelevant. It's imperative to remember that our most catastrophic impulses often start small, banal. Virality is compartmentalization, turning the complexities of life into decontextualized snapshots. It is a fun way to pass the time. It is a terrible way to run a society.

Is Bub happier being a famous cat? Or would she be just as happy eating jellied steer anus out of an old yogurt container and never, not once, seeing the inside of BuzzFeed HQ? Bub's answers—"probably not" and "probably," probably—are, for the purposes of this essay, less significant than ours: "Who fucking cares?"

The problem isn't that people have latent biases that manifest in unexpected ways; it's that we, as a society, are fundamentally allergic to examining those biases and holding ourselves accountable.

Bub opened the gates to a flood of feline misfits: Maru, who loves boxes; Honey Bee, who has no eyes; Kylo, who looks like Adam Driver; Lazarus, with the cleft palate; the late Colonel Meow, eulogized by TMZ under the violently disrespectful headline "Colonel Meow: Death Caused by Heart CAT-ASTROPHY"; and, of course, Grumpy Cat (RIP).

Grumpy Cat harrumphed into the public eye on September 22, 2012, when her owner's brother, Bryan Bundesen, posted a photo on Reddit with the caption "Meet grumpy cat." It was a media landscape not much more sophisticated than the one that had welcomed Lil Bub, but with one major difference: we already knew that a cat could be famous. And this cat got very famous. When she died in 2019, the *New York Times* ran a news story. The *Today* show ran a segment and displayed a Grumpy Cat meme: "I AM NOW IN HEAVEN. I HATE IT."

Grumpy Cat, like Lil Bub, was small, with facial deformities that gave her the look of a permanent frown. She was very adorable. She was also instantly meme-able, affording her a virality far beyond "look at this funny cat." Image macros featuring Grumpy Cat's scowl with captions such as "I HAD FUN ONCE; IT WAS AWFUL" and simply

"NO." They were inescapable on social media within what felt like hours. Merchandising and endorsement deals would quickly follow—T-shirts, mugs, plush toys, comic books, Halloween costumes, a bottled iced coffee called Grumppuccino, a contract with Friskies—bolstered by a large-scale PR campaign orchestrated by celebrity cat manager Ben Lashes.

Abruptly, in the midst of the flurry to Monetize! This! Cat!, the internet threw a wrench into the works, as it so often does. Someone noticed that this cat's owners called it Tard.

I want to quickly mention that what follows is my own personal conspiracy theory and I don't know shit. But also, unrelatedly, I am very smart.

The abbreviation "tard" is easily recognizable to anyone who has spent time online or the playground or the Thanksgiving table with their shittiest uncle within the last thirty years or so. Tard, on the face of it, is short for "r*tard" or "r*tarded," unless you believe that Grumpy Cat was named after the sixth most upvoted definition on Urban Dictionary: "A word used in Steinbeck's Grapes of Wrath; tired. 'Granma's just "tard.–Ma." Every other definition is a variation on the first: "Adjective used to describe one so r*tarded, they do not deserve the 're.'" (Housekeeping note: The R word is a slur, and I will be censoring it throughout. If you don't think it's a slur, and you think this is silly, consider that it costs you nothing to err on the side of care.)

I remember the rise of "tard," back when we were still pretending that it was okay to use the R word as long as we were "just joking" and referring to someone neurotypical. ("You don't call r*tarded people r*tards," Michael Scott said on the NBC sitcom *The Office* in 2006, then watched by millions of people, to no major blowback, "you call your friends r*tards when they're being r*tarded.") "Tard" on its own was the epithet with a little youthful flair; as a suffix it allowed anyone to add some ableism to their political agenda or Twitter beef ("libtard," "fucktard").

Come on. We know what it means. Come on. We are adults and our brains are oxygenated and we live in the world. We have all been here this whole time! Come on! *We know!*

The deduction seemed obvious to many people: Grumpy Cat was named Tard because she was a special needs cat. Her face was different. She had a flat affect and some trouble with her legs. Tard means r*tarded.

When the anti-Tard backlash, predictably, body slammed the Grumpy Cat money machine, the damage control was swift. Her owner, Tabatha Bundesen—presumably coached by celebrity cat manager Ben Lashes—released a statement explaining that, funny story, big misunderstanding, she'd let her young daughter name the cat, and the child chose, of all strange things, "Tardar Sauce," because she thought this cat's orangish fur resembled Red Lobster's signature orangish tartar sauce. And because children don't know how to spell "tartar" and Tabatha, I guess, got the name in writing from her toddler (?) and didn't bother to correct her, Tardar Sauce it was! And I guess nobody in their family or circle of friends had ever heard the word "tard" used as a slur, so the nickname raised no red flags whatsoever! Just think—if the kid had been better at spelling, the cat's nickname would have been Tart! And the whole goof would have been avoided! Because this story is very true! I guess!

Come on!!!

But brazenly retrofitting a celebrity cat with a backstory to dodge charges of ableism and keep that Friskies money flowing—if that is, indeed, what happened—isn't even the most irritating part of this whole situation. The most irritating part is how uncritically people believed the story. Or, maybe, pretended to believe it. The public ate it up. People wanted to be able to look at pictures of Grumpy Cat's cute, grumpy face so passionately that they chose to believe a very odd and suspiciously convenient tale we'd all just watched be conjured in real time.

The website Mental Floss regurgitated Grumpy Cat's origin story wholesale in 2019:

> Crystal came up with Grumpy Cat's real name—Tardar Sauce—which was inspired by two things: Grumpy's original orangish coloring ("She thought

> Grumpy looked like Tartar sauce," Tabatha said) and the fact that, at the time, Tabatha was waitressing at Red Lobster and had just made Crystal try the stuff. "She was like, 'Ew, no!' and I said 'Honey, you have to try it! It goes with fish!'" So it was fresh in her mind when the kitten was born.

I'm sorry. I just cannot buy this.

Similarly, Grumpy Cat's Wikipedia entry lists her name as Tardar Sauce without question, but there's some refreshing dissent on the Talk page (caveat that I do not know any of these anonymous users but I am extrapolating my opinion of their moral characters based on how hard they agree with me):

"Am I the only one to believe that the name of the cat 'Tard' is a retcon because the reality would be politically incorrect? Who names their cat 'Tartar Sauce'??" asks a keen-eyed anonymous user.

"The cat's name is 'Tardar Sauce.' It seems reasonable to call her 'Tard' for short," responds a credulous Grumpy Cat shill.

"I agree with the OP, I believe it's a retcon. It's not 'tardar sauce,' it's 'tar**t**ar sauce.' The word 'Tard,' however, *is* an actual slang for mental ret*rdation. There's no proof, but I've always felt something was fishy about the name and the explanation of it," says a genius.

The most gullible man in the world adds, "Sorry, but the spelling is with a 'd,' not a 't.' People give all kinds of unusual names and spellings of those unusual names to their animals."

And Geoff, a true king, brings it home: "Dude, of course it's a revision of history. They named the cat 'Tard,' because omg lol, the cat looks mentally r*tarded, then it became famous, and then they were like 'Oh crap, we now have a famous cat with a *really* offensive name. Quick, come up with some semi-plausible modification to the name and a story about how she got that name!' Honestly, I wish more people would call out the owners for the name: it's not cool."

YES, GEOFF. YES. GEOFF 2020.

Wikipedia might need "reliable sources" to add a detail to the main page, but I don't. It is my 100 percent certain, deeply held opinion that THIS FUCKING CAT'S NAME IS R*TARD AND THESE PEOPLE, WITH COLLUSION FROM CELEBRITY CAT MANAGER BEN LASHES, COVERED IT UP FOR THE MEGABUCKS.

Americans are addicted to plausible deniability. If we can't even think critically about something as relatively insignificant as an internet cat or admit that a person might give a pet an offensive name or apologize honestly for small, careless slights, how are we ever going to reckon with the fact that our country was built by slaves on land stolen from people on whom we perpetrated a genocide? What the fuck are we going to do?

Our propensity for always, always, always choosing what is comfortable over what is right helped pave the road to this low and surreal moment in US history.

In October 2017, BuzzFeed News published a truly astonishing exposé on the so-called alt-right, the youth-driven, archconservative online movement that is at least partly responsible for Donald Trump's rise to power and has been an indispensable siege engine in his war on truth. An unnamed entity sent BuzzFeed a cache of emails from the former Breitbart editor and alt-right figurehead Milo Yiannopoulos—Steve Bannon's protégé—revealing that Yiannopoulos had been working intimately with white nationalist leaders to normalize radical far-right ideology, particularly among disaffected white youth.

Yiannopoulos has experienced something of a fall from grace—both mainstream and fringe—since 2017. After videos surfaced in which Yiannopoulos appeared to endorse sexual relationships between thirteen-year-old boys and adult men ("they can be hugely positive experiences," he said), Simon & Schuster canceled the publication of his memoir and he was forced to resign from Breitbart. But back in 2015 and 2016, when the leaked emails were written, Yiannopoulos was the most popular writer at a right-wing website during a right-wing groundswell, a celebrated figure who held the ear of a future adviser to the president of the United States.

In a bizarre personal twist, one of the leaked emails exposed a connection between Yiannopoulos and an ostensibly feminist writer named Mitchell Sunderland, then employed at Broadly, Vice Media's women's section. "Please mock this fat feminist," Sunderland wrote to Yiannopoulos in May 2016, with a link to one of my articles. That email corroborated two things that feminist writers have been insisting, fruitlessly, for years: one, that the abuse we endure daily on social media isn't just a natural, inevitable by-product of the internet but a coordinated, politically motivated silencing campaign; and two, that even left-wing media failed to take us seriously when we insisted that Yiannopoulos was more than a clown. It was easier (and far more satisfying if you were already of the opinion that feminists are annoying) to believe that we were just hysterical.

The alt-right has always thrived on obfuscation and disinformation. A few of its founding factions include a misogynist hate movement that insists it's a good-faith crusade for journalistic ethics and free speech, multiple white supremacist hate movements that insist they're simply passionate about "Western culture," and the disfigured (or perhaps unmasked) remains of the Republican Party, which has long hidden its ruthless determination to enrich the richest at the expense of the poorest behind lies about "small government" and "personal responsibility."

How did such a conglomerate of transparent bigots achieve enough mainstream credibility to win the White House? Well, because they said, over and over, that they weren't bigots—the "nu-uh" defense.

And people believed them or pretended to because it was easier, because the alternative meant admitting some complicity in four centuries of American horrors. But my taxes are too high. But Michael Brown was no angel. But I'm not racist. But I *like* the cat.

The alt-right insisted it was not racist even as its swastika-clad minions marched on Charlottesville, Virginia, in August 2017 and the president it helped elect relentlessly demonized Muslims and Mexican immigrants and trafficked in vile stereotypes about the lives of black Americans. The alt-right insisted it was not sexist even as its online foot soldiers harassed feminist writers into hiding and its president bragged about committing sexual assault. Plausible deniability was the alt-right's Trojan horse, and the media ate it up, running puff pieces that cast Yiannopoulos as an outrageous cad and interviewing neo-Nazis to get "their side" of the story.

The BuzzFeed emails laid waste to it all. There was no longer any remotely justifiable reason to suggest that Yiannopoulos's popularity among neo-Nazis could merely be a coincidence or, by extension, that white male supremacy is not the defining principle of Trumpism. Yiannopoulos, working under the orders of the man who would become the president's chief strategist, was soliciting ideological guidance from overt white supremacists, including Andrew Auernheimer, known as weev, of the neo-Nazi website Daily Stormer. Yiannopoulos's contacts also advised him on how to more effectively mask his propaganda—to delight and whip up his base without alienating the center. (Remember when we thought the center could be alienated? Cute!)

None of this is new, of course, except for the scale of it. Trump sailed into the political sphere in 2011 on a gale of dog whistles, exploiting Americans' antiblack hostility without ever quite calling Barack Obama a racial slur. He just wasn't sure about Obama's citizenship, he said. He just wanted proof, he said, and didn't the American people deserve it? He was just a reality TV star asking in TV interviews and on Twitter for the president of the United States to show his papers.

Of course, to anyone with even the remotest grasp of nuance, context, US history, or good faith, Trump's racism has always been glaring, as has Yiannopoulos's. But as long as Trump insists, again and again, that he's the "least racist person," that's plausible deniability enough for millions of Americans. Even that BuzzFeed exposé, explicitly demonstrating a direct chain of communication from organized white nationalists to President Trump, changed nothing.

After a frenzied few days on Twitter, the discourse moved on with a shrug, because real change takes work and blood. *On the one hand, there's what we can plainly see in front of us with our own eyes. On the other hand, he says he's not racist!*

When faced with a choice between an incriminating truth or a flattering lie, America's ruling class has been choosing the lie for four hundred years.

White Americans hunger for plausible deniability and swaddle themselves in it and always have—for the sublime relief of deferred responsibility, the soft violence of willful ignorance, the barbaric fiction of rugged individualism. The worst among us have deployed it to seduce and herd the vast, complacent center: It's okay. You didn't do anything wrong. You earned everything you have. Benefiting from genocide is fine if it was a long time ago. The scientists will figure out climate change. The cat's name is Tardar Sauce.

We have to kick this addiction if we're going to give our children any kind of future.

In August 2016, a *Nightline* producer asked if I'd be willing to appear in a segment about internet trolling alongside Yiannopoulos, and I reluctantly agreed, on the condition that I could discuss online harassment's dire political ramifications—which, in just a few months, would help put Trump in the White House. "Milo and his followers are defending the status quo," I wrote in an email. "They are explicitly attacking women and people of color in order to squash social justice movements. They are anti-Semitic, transphobic, misogynist white supremacists, no matter how much Milo couches it in his naughty scoundrel schtick." I had no idea, at the time, how right I was about to be.

When the piece aired, the text under my face—the chyron—read "Trolling Victim." Any political analysis I'd provided was cut in favor of a cursory description of mean things trolls have said to me. That's the story they wanted—the simple story, the easy story, the story audiences like. Trolls mean! Women cry! Just like all the other "trolling victims," I was a spectacle, entertainment for the masses as much as I'd been entertainment for the trolls. The truth, as ever, would have been a buzzkill.

The cat isn't the problem. Even the cat's name isn't the problem, though the name is terrible. The name is just people needing to grow. The problem is the story about the name (if the Tardar Sauce backstory is indeed a fabrication) and the public's eagerness to believe it; the problem is people weaseling out of the growth. We are addicted to not being inconvenienced by reality, even in the most mundane circumstances. We just want to have everything.

Say that I am correct about this whole thing. If Grumpy Cat's owners did, in fact, name their cat Tard, and then opted to respond transparently when called out, what's the worst that could have happened? If they'd issued a sincere apology, renamed the cat, and made a charitable donation, would the public have stopped thinking the cat was cute? Would we have stopped buying mugs and calendars and bottled iced coffee? Even if they hadn't done that—if they'd said, "Yeah, the cat's name is Tard and we think it's cool and we stand by it"—Tard would have been doing drop-in sets at the Comedy Cellar to standing ovations within a month.

If we're going to pull our country and our planet back from the brink, we have to start living in the truth. We have to start calling things by their real names: racism is racism, sexism is sexism, mistakes are mistakes, and they can be rectified if we do the work.

We escape into home renovation shows because it's easier to imagine an apolitical world where everyone can afford a house than it is to actually build that world. We gobble up cable news' insistence that both sides of an argument are equally valid and *South Park*'s insistence that both sides are equally stupid, because taking a firm stand on anything opens us up to criticism. We live willingly within the lies constructed by abortion opponents, enforcing shame and stigma around a basic human freedom, because we're afraid to say the word *abortion* out loud. We kept letting Adam Sandler make more movies after *Little Nicky*, because white men are allowed to fail spectacularly and keep their jobs.

We cannot protect women from intimate partner violence until we stop treating battered wives as discrete hourlong plotlines instead of interconnected points on a millennia-long continuum. We cannot achieve racial equality until we stop giving twenty-two-year-old male comedians who believe in "reverse racism" as much credence in the "discourse" as we give black scholars and academics. We can't save ourselves until we get comfortable with discomfort. The truth hurts. But the future we're building without it will hurt more.

Is Adam Sandler Funny?

I turned thirty-seven right in the midst of a series of intense deadlines—aka the "Watching 'Zelda: Breath of the Wild' Boss Fight Tutorial Videos on YouTube and Justifying It 'Because I'm Eating'" phase of the writing process, a technique I'm sure you're all familiar with from *J. D. Salinger: A Life*—which meant that I could not spare one spring second for joy, cake, sunshine, or friendship on the official first day of my late thirties (knife emoji, skull emoji, coffin emoji).

Instead of partying, I had to figure out a way to get some work done in a slightly more celebratory style than my usual routine, which is, obviously, hunching over a laptop going positively rodential on a jumbo bag of dill pickle–flavored sunflower seeds with my chin resting on an upside-down Coke Zero bottle I've wedged into my cleavage. Does that sound like a birthday girl to you? Does it even sound, technically, like a *Homo sapien*?

For my DIY Take Your Thirty-Seven-Year-Old Rat-Woman to Work Day, I really snazzed it up. I took a hot shower and put on my coziest jammies. My husband made me a jalapeño bagel with cream cheese, tomato, and cayenne (SEND ME $1,000 FOR THIS BITCHING HACK). I swaddled myself in the number one couch blanket and refused to share it with my shivering family. My mom brought over a coconut crème pie and my gift: three canisters of pepper spray, because in this wild freelance writer's life, a lot can happen between the bed and the toilet and the other toilet and back to the bed. And I did something I'd been putting off for months, the very last piece in a very important part of this book:

I watched *Little Nicky.*

"Is Adam Sandler Funny?" was the very first chapter I conceived of for this book, years ago now, after I stumbled across *Billy Madison* on cable and found it absolutely baffling. Was this really the thing we had worshipped all those years? Why does a grown woman want to fuck a man who goes to kindergarten and talks like a baby? Am I hallucinating, or are there no jokes in this at all?

My intention was to watch every single Adam Sandler movie ever made—or at least the *Adam Sandler* Adam Sandler movies, if you know what I mean. The ones where Adam Sandler *does the voice* and Adam Sandler's friends are played by those three dudes who are always in Adam Sandler movies (Allen Covert, Peter Dante, and Jonathan

Loughran, if you want to look them up and go, "Oh, yeah, those guys") and Rob Schneider plays some sort of bewildered ethnic clown. Usually a Dennis Dugan joint with a Dennis Dugan cameo.

I was genuinely curious about what I'd find. *Billy Madison* is considered one of the true Sandler classics—I had fond enough memories of it from my youth—but rewatching it, I just couldn't connect. Perhaps it's an inevitable by-product of time and perspective: it's hard to laugh at Sandler as an adult woman when you're suddenly, painfully aware of how he helped shape the adult men around you.

I didn't actually manage to watch or rewatch every Adam Sandler movie. I didn't get to *Mr. Deeds, Anger Management, 50 First Dates, The Longest Yard, Click, Grown Ups, Grown Ups 2, Blended, Pixels, The Ridiculous 6, The Do-over,* or any of Sandler's new Netflix content. Which sounds like a big lapse, until you consider that I did watch *Happy Gilmore, Billy Madison, The Waterboy, The Wedding Singer, I Now Pronounce You Chuck and Larry, You Don't Mess with the Zohan, Jack and Jill,* and *That's My Boy,* which you haven't even heard of, *and* I listened to Sandler's multiplatinum 1993 comedy album *They're All Gonna Laugh at You!* in its entirety, AND it turns out I can still recite most of "Fatty McGee" from memory, from back when I used to think it was important to signal to people that it was okay to make fun of fat people around me because I'm the cool kind of fat person who knows I deserve shame.

So if you are tempted to pooh-pooh my expertise in matters of Sandler, kindly refer above to the part where I said I WATCHED *LITTLE NICKY* ON MY BIRTHDAY.

I was a little *Saturday Night Live* freak growing up. I recorded it off the TV and watched the tapes until they wore out, committing even the most middling, now-forgotten sketches to memory. I can't isolate now how I felt about Sandler then, because that wasn't how it worked. I loved *comedy*, and so I loved Sandler.* He was part of a whole, a big, important part. I couldn't separate him from whatever alchemy made *SNL* so special any more than I could separate my head from my neck.

When Sandler left *SNL* and started making movies, I followed, along with the rest of the world. But, in hindsight, a part of me always felt that those movies weren't *for me*. I never connected with them in quite the same way as my male peers did. I found parts to love, anyway, and jokes to quote, and I pored over the IMDb pages until I knew every bit actor, because what else was I going to do? I loved comedy. I didn't think about it at the time, but there was no Adam Sandler for girls—no one making blockbuster comedies about girls having fun and being gross, no one telling us that we were good the way we were and the joke was on the rest of the world. We took what we could get.

---

* Except for Opera Man. WHAT IS THE JOKE???

My curiosity flared when I flipped past *Billy Madison* that day, so many years later, and thought—wait, do I hate this? Is this why men my age don't know how to fold laundry? Is this why I once cried over a man with a handlebar mustache who slept on a bare mattress in an unfinished basement?

Here commences the results section of my study. (I do want to issue one caveat, which is that Steve Buscemi is an angel in every single one of these movies, even the ones in which he does not appear.)

Happy Gilmore (1996)

The golf one. Adam Sandler is an ice hockey player whose only talent is using his impotent rage to hit the puck really really extremely hard. He gets fired from hockey and decides to try golf. Surprise! Turns out he's the greatest golfer alive! He beats the shit out of Bob Barker, and then in the end he wins one golf jacket and one Julie Bowen.

Billy Madison (1995)

Adam Sandler goes back to elementary school and fucks his hot adult teacher even though he pisses his pants and talks in a baby voice and all his friends are four. He is the best at Academic Decathlon. Surprise.

Little Nicky (2000)

Little Nicky starts with Jon Lovitz, orange, sitting on a tree limb watching a woman undress through her bedroom window. At first I thought, "Oh, I see, he must be a lil devil from Hell who came up to Earth to be DIRTY," because I knew vaguely that the movie was about devils and the man is brightly illuminated and eating fried chicken out of a picnic basket balanced precariously in a tree and talking at full volume about a mom's jugs while she is like two feet away. But then the mom spies him and screams, and Jon Lovitz falls out of the tree and dies and goes to Hell. He was just a mortal peeper all along! A hilarious, hilarious sex criminal.

In hell, to pay for his penis crime, Satan sentences Lovitz to be raped eternally by a giant bird. Ever notice how men's idea of Hell is always rape? (Man, wait till they hear about Earth!) Other punishments meted out by *Little Nicky*'s Satan: Adolf Hitler—dressed as a French maid, because aren't women's clothes humiliating?—has a pineapple shoved up his asshole every day. Satan gets mad at his butler, Kevin Nealon, and makes Kevin Nealon grow tits on his head, because women's anatomy is humiliating, and then Kevin Nealon has to get raped by Rodney Dangerfield every day because of his tit head! Men's Hell is to be a woman.

Nicky is the youngest son of Academy Award nominee Harvey Keitel, the Devil, who is getting ready to retire and trying to decide which of his evil children should inherit his bad kingdom. But instead he's like "SIKE, you all suck" and decides to stay the Devil for another ten thousand years. This causes his two terrible sons to sneak out of Hell to go and make their own Hell on Earth. It falls to Nicky—despite the fact that he is, for all practical purposes, a dead snail—to go up top and try to stop them.

A major engine of comedy in *Little Nicky* is Nicky's culture shock upon arriving in New York City, because he does not know about common Earth things such as infrastructure, food, and money. For instance, after being hit by a train and waking up back in Hell, he says, "I got killed by this big light that was attached to a lot of metal," but then later he says (about something unrelated), "I'll have to take a mulligan on this one." You know what a mulligan is but you don't know what a train is? You don't know what a bus is but you understand the sentence "Your father gave me some deposit money for a place on the Upper East Side, but I misplaced it"? I hate you!

It turns out that the only way Nicky can save both Earth and Hell from his demon brothers is to harness the power of his seething, repressed, hellish anger. A good message, especially for boys! Nicky has no discernible skills, intellect, charisma, sense of humor, ambition, kindness, or personality, but he manages to skate by just well enough to get literally everything he wants. At the end, he fucks Patricia Arquette and beats the entire Harlem Globetrotters at one-on-one.

The Wedding Singer (1998)

Some people think of *The Wedding Singer* as one of the better Adam Sandler films, and I used to too, but HOLY MOLY, were women not allowed to break up with men in the nineties! "When I think of you, Linda," Sandler famously sings of his ex, "I hope you fucking choke." Sandler plays a wedding singer who, *quelle surprise*, actually deserved to be a rock star. Drew Barrymore is precious, and Alexis Arquette deserved better from this world, but I wish every man in my generation hadn't been taught that it is well and good to wish death upon women who leave you. Counterpoint: Women have free will! Bye!

You Don't Mess with the Zohan (2008)

I feel as though this movie puts a lot of faith in Americans' awareness of Israeli stereotypes. Is it common knowledge that Mossad agents really really love hacky-sack? Regardless, Adam Sandler is the best at it, and fighting, and hair.

Big Daddy (1999)

This is the other one everyone remembers as pretty good. But somehow we *don't* remember that the big joke of this movie is "What if a MAN had to do the stuff that WOMEN do!?!??!?" Adam Sandler takes in (kidnaps) a small child and teaches him how to piss in public, cause Rollerbladers mortal injury, and brutally degrade Leslie Mann for working at Hooters while putting herself through law school. Just when you think Sandler might not be the best at something in one of his movies, a supporting character who is a lawyer mentions something about a tough case and Sandler says, "You could always sue them under the corrupt standards and practices act," and everyone is blown away because it turns out that he is the greatest lawyer on Earth even though he works in a tollbooth.

I Now Pronounce You Chuck & Larry (2007)
Glaringly homophobic even when it came out, a time when it was still socially acceptable to call shirts "f*ggy" for being pink.

Jack and Jill (2011)
Jack (Sandler), the most brilliant and revolutionary advertising executive ever to trod 'pon Gaia's green crust, has to impersonate his annoying twin sister, Jill (also Sandler), so that he can use her carnal magnetism to trick Al Pacino (as himself) into rapping in a Dunkin' Donuts commercial. That is the real plot.

That's My Boy (2012)
I didn't even know that *That's My Boy* existed, and it was not on my list for this project until I accidentally came across it while flipping channels (yes, I have regular cable like a MOLDERING CORPSE) and was captivated. A light

romp inspired by the foibles of famous child rapist Mary Kay Letourneau,* *That's My Boy* is the story of a boy (Adam Sandler) who fathers a child (Andy Samberg) with one of his middle school teachers, then proceeds to name the baby Han Solo, give it a large tattoo, and, on account of being twelve, is surprisingly just not that good of a dad in general. After years of estrangement, Sandler shows up at the now grown-up Samberg's wedding, pretending to miss his boy but actually perpetrating a wicked scheme to obtain $50 grand from a tabloid and thereby avoid debtor's prison.

In the end, it's all fine because it turns out that Samberg's fiancée is fucking her own brother and then a big fat man named Tubby Tuke, whom Sandler had bet on as a joke, accidentally wins the Boston Marathon. Adam Sandler goes back to banging grannies and basically being a professional baseball player. A classic American tale.

***The Waterboy* (1998)**

Sandler is Bobby Boucher, a "socially inept" waterboy with extreme anger problems (again), who you think is only going to be the best at knowing about water but also turns out to be the strongest and fastest linebacker of all time.

---

* Once I was shopping at the downtown Seattle Nordstrom with my mother and noticed that hometown hero Mary Kay Letourneau was in line directly in front of us, so I took my phone and typed "Mary Kay Letourneau" and discreetly showed it to my mom, and she squinted at it and said, "MARY . . . KAY . . . LETOURNEAU?"

Even though he is "socially inept," Fairuza Balk wants to eat that ass like a dog on a litter box. Then the Mud Dogs win the Bourbon Bowl and Bobby is MVP and it is strongly implied that he drops out of college to join the NFL. Kathy Bates does her best.

I have managed to scientifically isolate the seven essential components of any classic Adam Sandler movie:

1. Adam Sandler seems like he's the boy who's kind of a loser, BUT WEALLY HE'S DA BEST BOY and it's the wesponsible guy who's BAD!
2. Adam Sandler talks in a funny voice and/or is a simpleton of unknown provenance.
3. Adam Sandler has severe anger problems, which benefit him.
4. Adam Sandler seems like just a generic dork, but secretly he is the strongest and best at a sport or trade.
5. Adam Sandler urinates in public.
6. Adam Sandler behaves as a giant baby would behave.
7. Adam Sandler is a deeply, deeply unappealing creature, a true bare-minimum kind of human, yet a beautiful woman is hornily drawn to him and yearns to be his bride.

There's a lot of bad in here—women as door prizes for male growth, women lusting ravenously after men who offer them nothing, women shamed for their sexuality, women punished for rejecting men, women forever on the margins. It is so normal for white men to fail upward that it skews our perception of what is good. Can you imagine if Ellen Cleghorne had made a *Little Nicky*? You think she'd get to make seventy-seven more movies after that? You think she'd get to make *one*?

I assumed that this chapter would deliver me to some big fat feminist dunk about how Adam Sandler movies indoctrinated a generation of boys into the notion that the world was theirs for the taking whether they bothered to grow up or try hard or do a good job or not. Any random shithead can be the best at a sport, without training or dedication. A woman is a thing you get, not a person you get to know.

And I'm sure that message did filter into the collective subconscious of my generation's boys to some degree, perhaps to all of our detriment. I mean, look at the world around us. But it can also be true that Sandler was a product of his time, reflecting the values of his time, just trying to make people laugh in the parlance of his time. The notion that men are the center of the world and women are supporting characters was certainly not invented in 1998. For me, I guess, the crux lies less in the movies themselves and more in the emptiness around them. I don't begrudge the straight white boys their abundance; I just wish the rest of us had had the same.

In the last few weeks of writing this book, while I was living in New York and simultaneously working on season two of *Shrill* the show, sweet Aidy Bryant offered me tickets to an *SNL* taping. The host, by pure coincidence, through some spasm of divinity that I don't believe in but clearly should, was Adam Sandler.

And, man, I fucking cried! I cried my ass off.

The episode had an emotional charge from the start. It wasn't just me; from my seat I could see *SNL* cast members crying, too, hugging each other in the wings, thinking, maybe, about where they had come from and what lay ahead. It was out of nostalgia partially for Sandler himself—I am more attached to him than I'd thought—and partially for the legacy of his era, for the sense memory of being young, for the years when you can love things so purely without complication. It was watching Sandler, fifty-two, tired, process his return to an old home, where he himself had once been young, in a time when it must have felt as though everything was happening for him, finally, and Chris Farley was still alive. I didn't even mind that he did Opera Man.*

---

* I did mind. Missing: the joke of Opera Man, $200,000,000 reward.

But even in the fun and the nostalgia, you could feel that it was a little different for the boys. There was a giddiness radiating from *SNL*'s male cast members, as though they were truly in Heaven—in one sketch, "Sandler Family Reunion," one after another got to do his Sandler impression for Sandler, and of course they all had one. They were kids again for a night as well as the men those kids had dreamed of becoming, and it was something magic because Sandler was *for them*—in the worlds he constructed, comedy boys were king.

Girls deserved more than a glow reflected.

Ted Bundy Was Not Charming—Are You High?

For as long as I can remember, I've been terrified that a man was going to sneak into my house and murder me. Actually, "convinced" might be a more accurate word than "terrified," but I don't want to say "convinced" because I am at the same time totally dismissive of the supernatural and extremely superstitious. I don't think jinxing things is real, but I DO NOT jinx things. Why risk it? Just a few weeks ago I was sitting in my hotel lobby in New York City reading Jason Mantzoukas's Wikipedia entry, and then Jason Mantzoukas walked by me! Who knows what's possible! Plus, if you say things such as "I'm convinced I will get serial killed" and then by coincidence you do get serial killed, it becomes a whole thing in your *Dateline*. Keith Morrison is like "A beautiful young nymph. Haunted by visions. Of being? *Serial killed*. BuT ThEY wErE OnLy vIsIoNs . . . right? [plaintive glissando] WROOONG. One hot summer night. In a sleepy toooooown! Deep in the heart . . . of Texas. Those visions! Became all too reeeeeeeal."

Three asides on *Dateline* real quick: (1) It was either the husband, the ex-husband, or someone who wanted to fuck her but she turned him down. White cops always want it to be someone's possible ties to the Russian mob because their brother sold someone named Kazimir a boat in 1992, and it is never, ever that! It is never a global human trafficking ring! Eat it, white guys, you love weird sex murder. (2) The only foolproof way to murder your wife is to take her hiking and then VERY gently hip check her off a cliff. You can't hip check her too hard because the scientists can tell the trajectory! The scientists always measure! (3) All *Dateline* correspondents are my children, but here is my ranking of them in order of how much I love my children: Keith Morrison, Josh Mankiewicz, Andrea Canning, Dennis Murphy.

I have to say it was a little annoying when, in January 2019, everyone on Earth suddenly became Ted Bundy experts because of Netflix's four-part documentary series *Conversations with a Killer: The Ted Bundy Tapes*. Like, excuse me, some of us have had the Wikipedia page "List of serial killers by number of victims" bookmarked since 2006, and it was only published in 2005. (Also a hot hot read: "List of fatal bear attacks in North America by decade.") Likewise, the great true crime podcast boom of Trump's America has been both an irritant and a boon. LIKE, YES, IT'S MY FOOD, FEED ME MY FOOD, BUT ALSO PLEASE ACKNOWLEDGE AND HONOR MY LIFELONG INTEREST IN SEXUAL KNIFE CRIME.

Something just occurred to me. Do cisgender men not spend absolutely every moment of their lives obsessed with the possibility of home invasion? Do they sleep soundly all through the night, *even if there is a noise*? Do they notice if they get home and the porch light is off but they are certain they turned the porch light on before they left? Do they think about giving up their lovely house, their porch, their garden, for a high-rise apartment because there are fewer points of entry? Do they consider going home from work early because they can't stop wondering if the wooden dowel in the basement window track has somehow come askew? Do they rehearse protocols for which heavy dresser they will shove in front of the bedroom door if they hear someone creaking up the hallway and lie awake at night wondering how thick particle board would need to be to stop bullets? What about particle board, a layer of folded sweaters, and then another piece of particle board with a faux wood-grain laminate? How easily and how far can one man shove one door, one fat woman, and one piece of an Ikea bedroom set? Could I survive a jump out of a second-story window? Should I aim for the tree or try to avoid the tree? Do fat people bounce better or hit harder?

I'm sure some men think of these things, of course. But is such vigilance, for them, as subconscious and involuntary as breathing? Is it constant, a processor whirring 24/7? Are they thinking about waking up with a man looming at the foot of the bed or pressing down on top of them? Or do they merely see a threat to their property, a territorial violation?

Does every day feel like a stay of execution?

Often, when I hear men speak about home invasion, it's not in the context of what an intruder might do to them but rather, in an almost fetishistic way, what they might do to an intruder. These men yearn to stand their ground, to have an excuse to use their arsenal, to find out what it feels like to kill another human being (and you know, in this morally bereft country, what color human being they're picturing).

Straight, white, cisgender men love to file serial killers under some darker subcategory of white male genius. It's easier to be titillated when fear is an abstraction. Ooh, BTK installed security systems so he could disarm them later. Isn't that smart? Gary Ridgway eluded the cops for twenty years. Bundy wore a fake cast! Diabolical! No, you dick lickers, they were fucking pathetic, opportunistic, incel losers who leveraged the staggering confidence that our society confers upon bare-minimum white men in order to get away with obliterating the lives of sexual objects they despised because they could not own them.

Much like Ada Lovelace, the inventor of the fucking computer.

It was interesting to observe the renewed national conversation about Bundy in light of another national obsession incubating at the time: the early stirrings of the 2020 presidential campaign.

Watching otherwise rational human beings rhapsodize about Bundy's "charm" and "brilliance" while furrowing their brows over Elizabeth Warren's dubious "likability" creates a particularly American kind of whiplash. The prevailing Bundy narrative has always hammered away at how "handsome" and "charismatic" the man was, but one would think that in 2019—if #MeToo brownshirts truly have the death grip on pop culture and justice that the whingeing class claims we do—someone might have red-flagged the canonization of a shitty rapist failure who murdered at least thirty women?

Ted Bundy was a mediocre student whom no one liked who failed at everything he ever tried to do except for exploiting women's socialization as caregivers in order to put them into vulnerable situations so he could take away their one single precious exquisite life.

Elizabeth Warren put herself through Rutgers Law School with a toddler at home, held endowed professorships at the University of Pennsylvania School of Law and Harvard Law School, became perhaps the most influential expert on bankruptcy law in the country, has been a

US senator since 2012, and is now arguably the most principled and policy-driven candidate in the fight to wrest power from a profligate dictator and lead Americans to help save our dying planet. Ugh, off-putting! I hate it when my mommy makes me brush my teeth! Far more likeably, Ted Bundy pretended to have a broken arm so he could rape, bludgeon, shoot, and stab women.

Things that DON'T make a (white) man unlikable:

Murdering
Stealing everyone's money
Grabbing women by the pussy
Cult leading
Making everyone in your cult commit suicide with you
Genocide
Being a DJ

Things that DO make a woman unlikable:

Voice
Body
Hair
Shoes
Kids
No kids
Sex
No sex

Money
No money
Inhale
Exhale
Metabolize food
Shed skin cells
Use muscles to move bones around
Do anything
Die

Likability is a con, and we're all falling for it. I watched Netflix and Hulu's dueling documentaries on the social media megascam Fyre Festival the same week that I got that Ted Bundy documentary in my craw. And, look, I am not saying that Fyre Festival CEO Billy McFarland is like a serial killer because he lured hundreds of nubile young influencers to a remote island with no food or shelter and then tooted off on a golden Jet Ski and left them to be eaten by wild pigs. (The lawyer says I have to clarify that he didn't LITERALLY do this.) I am saying that McFarland is like a serial killer because he is exactly as likable as Ted Bundy, yet somehow I had to watch two entire documentaries about how "charming" and "charismatic" he is.

I'm sorry. Is everyone on MDMA? And can I please have some?

Billy McFarland is the most obvious bumbling con-artist dumbass ever birthed by the universe. He's the guy who never helps on the group project. He's the bully's least memorable henchman. He's that kind of American rich kid who doesn't bother to learn more than one vowel. He looks like the producers spread peanut butter on his tongue and then had his audio dubbed by a frat guy halfway through dying of alcohol poisoning. He seems to be, to put it charitably, barely alive. If we're all made of star stuff, he's from the butt part of the star.

Sorry to be a mean bitch, but I am so fucking sick—FUCKING VIOLENTLY ILL—of having to watch good people be conned by smug simpletons who couldn't beat a dog at Candyland. Ted Bundy and Billy McFarland are both more charming than Donald Trump, and that boner pratfalled his way into becoming the most powerful man on earth. That guy? *That guy* is who brought us down?

One malicious side effect of Americans' bootstrap ethos (itself just a massive grift to empower the snickering rich) is that it conditions people to cheer at deregulation, to beg and plead for the removal of consumer protections. We are literally asking to be conned; we are a smorgasbord for the most unscrupulous and the least deserving. Being a giant fucking sucker is as American as school shootings.

The past few decades have been a tug-of-war over the benefit of the doubt. Black Lives Matter demands that white America adjust its assumptions about the inherent goodness of cops, about who looks like a criminal and who looks like a fine boy having a bad mental health day.

#MeToo demands we reexamine what credibility looks like—who gets to define it and mete it out, who gets to stride through the world assuming that they have it.

Institutional benefit of the doubt is monstrously powerful: any lie becomes an incantation, conjuring itself into truth. This is the foundation of Donald Trump's power.

"I am a handsome law student!"

"The Fyre Festival is real, and Kendall Jenner will be there!"

"I'm the least racist person you'll ever meet!"

To fund Fyre Festival, Billy McFarland called people and asked for millions of dollars, and people were like "Sure!" To not get caught, Ted Bundy just had to exist—multiple acquaintances reported him based on the police sketch, his brown Volkswagen, and his shitty personality, but cops thought that a "handsome" (no) "law student" (he got bored and stopped going) couldn't possibly be a murderer. I mean, you guys! The Michael Scott Paper Company was just a supply closet filled with cheese balls and it got a multimillion-dollar buyout from Dunder Mifflin! Men, would it kill you to say thank you once in a while?

There's a famous moment from the Bundy trial in 1979—a trial in which Bundy disrupted the proceedings repeatedly with outlandish disrespect to the court and to his victims—when judge Edward D. Cowart of Dade County, Florida, delivered Bundy's death sentence:

> The court finds that both of these killings were indeed heinous, atrocious, and cruel. And that they were extremely wicked, shockingly evil, vile and the product of a design to inflict a high degree of pain and utter indifference to human life. This court, independent of, but in agreement with the advisory sentence rendered by the jury does hereby impose the death penalty upon the defendant Theodore Robert Bundy. It is further ordered that on such scheduled date that you be put to death by a current of electricity, sufficient to cause your immediate death, and such current of electricity shall continue to pass through your body until you are dead.

I don't believe in the death penalty, but otherwise that seems pretty on point. Then Cowart went on:

> Take care of yourself, young man. I say that to you sincerely; take care of yourself. It is an utter tragedy for this court to see such a total waste of humanity, I think, as I've experienced in this courtroom.
>
> (*Wow, um, okay, J-Cow, maybe time to wrap it u—*)
>
> You're a bright young man. You'd have made a good lawyer and I would have loved to have you

practice in front of me, but you went another way, partner. I don't feel any animosity toward you. I want you to know that. Take care of yourself.

To recap:

Women: Just livin' life, going to college, having brown hair, swimming, helping the injured.

Ted Bundy: Murders thirty women (at least) because his peepee scrunched from being a massive shitty failure.

The legal system: BUNDY YOU ARE A GREAT MAN AND A GREAT LAWYER AND COULD BE OUR GREATEST PRESIDENT IF I'M BEING HONEST BUT UNFORTCH I GOTTA SENTENCE YOU TO DEATH ON ACCOUNT OF ALL THE MURDER AND WHATNOT SORRY BUDDY DANG I WISH I COULD HIRE YOU AS MY SON AND HECK YOU SHOULD BE DOING MY JOB, PARTNER! PS U MY HERO.

I wonder how many of the women Bundy murdered would have made good lawyers. I wonder how many female and minority lawyers Judge Cowart mentored in his lifetime.

This anecdote is often held up as evidence of Bundy's charisma—even the judge sentencing him to death was seduced by that smirk, that finger wave. But it is the most blatant, overwhelming evidence we have for the opposite. Men don't need charisma to succeed. It doesn't matter if men are likable, because men are people who do things, who don't have to ask first, whose potential has value even after it is squandered.

On the other hand, women.

Is there such a thing as a likable woman? Can you think of one?

And if she exists, could she be anything but the ultimate manifestation of everything we hate about the water we swim in, everything we're forced to be? Likability in a sexist, racist culture is not objective—it's compulsory femininity, the gender binary, invisible labor, whiteness, smallness, sweetness. It's letting them do it.

If someone is universally likable, I don't trust that person. That's the opposite of politics. I don't want a candidate that the alt-right likes. I don't want to have anything in common with George Zimmerman. A person's standard of likability is a reflection of his beliefs, and unfortunately, in this country, a whole lot of people believe that Donald Trump is not a racist shart in an eight-foot tie who is unqualified for literally every job except "lie down."

So no, excuse me, we will not play likability anymore. It's an endless runner—a game with no progress and no finish line—that women are expected to chase, that keeps us from doing the real work, accruing the real power.

Chasing likability has been one of women's biggest setbacks, by design. I don't know that rejecting likability will get us anywhere, but I know that embracing it has gotten us nowhere.

"Witch" is something we call a woman who demands the benefit of the doubt, who speaks the truth, who punctures the con, who kills your joy if your joy is killing. A witch has power and power in women isn't likable, it's ugly, cartoonish. But to not assert our power—even if we fail—is to let them do it. This new truth telling, this witchcraft of ours, by definition cannot be likable. We cannot pander or wait for consensus; the world is too big and complicated and rigged. We are saying the things that people don't like, the only truly "edgy" things; that is the point.

Someone will always pop up to say, "You would be more effective if you were nicer." "You would have a more receptive audience if you adjusted your tone." "You catch more flies with honey." Well, I don't want flies. The most likable woman in the world is crawling with fucking flies.

How to Be a Girl

It's become a national sport to stereotype millennials[*]—we're lazy, we're entitled, instead of saving for retirement we're forever getting trampled by bison while trying to take selfies—because, sure, when you've set the world on complete fucking fire, why not spend your twilight years roasting your own grandchildren over the smoldering debris of their dreams?

But people always miss the number one most typical classic one weird trick about millennials, which is that older millennials like me, people who were born during Ronald Reagan's first term, have a singular great, passionate love above all else. Greater than avocado toast, greater than the *DuckTales* theme, greater than gender-swapped *Game*

---

* The Pew Research Center says that millennials are the generation born between 1981 and 1996, and I was born in 1982, which means that I AM ONE. I AM YOUNG. NO ONE CAN TELL ME I'M NOT YOUNG.

of Thrones characters reimagined as Disney princesses, greater than never owning property, greater than selling our plasma so we can make our student loan payments, greater even than being called a special snowflake for asking not to be raped by future Supreme Court justices.

Millennials. LOVE. Board game–based Cold War murder mystery sex farces chockablock with J. Edgar Hoover references. Bing bang bong! If you don't know that, then you don't know millennials, sweetie!

My best friend and I watched the movie *Clue* on VHS probably twice a week, every week, between 1987 and 1990, when I moved from Thousand Oaks to Seattle to teach a new city's children to accuse their grandmothers of being *in flagrante delicto.* Even then I knew that my love was weird. *Clue* did not feel like a kids' movie, and I did not even really like the board game Clue that much! It's so boring!

Professor Plum was disgusting and Mr. Boddy was so creepy, and it always bugged me that the actor who played Mr. Boddy picked "Lee Ving" to be his stage name. Lee Ving? Leaving? How is that a cool name? If you're going to change your name to be a word, you should go all the way with it, like "Bea Nanners" for a girl or "Harry Bunzmuncher" for a boy. Right? Also, what's a red herring?

Nevertheless, I was HORNY FOR *CLUE* from a young age until an old age. And when I grew up and started working for the internet—which is nothing if not a bunch of early-eighties millennials making lists of stuff they liked when they were eight, declaring they "feel old," and then turning to Nazism—I discovered something incredible: I wasn't alone, not remotely. *Clue* was HOT. Among people who turned twenty-nine in 2011, Martin Mull was more popular than Jesus.

I do get it. *Clue* is titillating, both sexwise and scarywise; the physical comedy is better than the jokes, and the jokes are good! It is really, really funny when the candlestick falls on Wadsworth's head. Tim Curry!!! And the gimmicky triple ending was like Choose Your Own Adventure except with just sitting there instead of choosing! Millennial-nip for the listless!

All of which is to say, I gave *Clue* a lot. My time, my love, my brain space, my video store rental fees. *Clue*, in turn, gave me something back: my first inkling of myself as a woman situated somewhere on a scary, hierarchical, baffling, shifting matrix of women.

There are four main women in *Clue* (I am excluding the cook, who immediately gets stabbed, and the singing telegram girl, who immediately gets shot). There are Yvette, the maid, who is a French sex goof; Mrs. White, who is a small and beautiful female separatist ice queen; Miss Scarlet, who is fricking glamorous as hell and a sexy madam in emerald satin who always has a horny innuendo in the chamber. And then there's Mrs. Peacock, who is wearing an entire natural history museum and constantly screaming.

I remember, as a child, looking from each of these women to the next, and trying to figure out which kind of woman I might grow up to be. I was NOT an Yvette, no offense. Mrs. White, no, very assertive. Miss Scarlet, I wished.

Hmm.

Hrm.

I was Mrs. Peacock. Okay? At age eight, the closest analogue I could find for myself in my favorite movie—a movie with more female characters than most—was a corrupt senator's wife who was older than my father and dressed like a Rainforest Cafe. An extremely hot and successful vibe to take into sixth grade!*

In middle school I got a new favorite movie, *Reality Bites*, and with it a new taxonomy. There are actually just two types of women, I decided: Winona Ryders and Janeane Garofalos. I would never, ever be a Winona, so I supposed I must be a Janeane. (Other things discovered around the same time that I would never be: a Shalom Harlow, a Brad from *Hey Dude*, a Delia's model, or a Penny from *Dirty Dancing*. Or a Baby from *Dirty Dancing*. Probably not even a Lisa. *Maybe* a watermelon.)

That's untrue, of course, and I know it now. Humanity is a great, messy striation with infinite metrics for beauty

* Who am I kidding with this bullshit, anyway—I'm the cook. PROUDLY. PROUD COOK.

and value; we do not actually come in "kinds." But what I took from *Reality Bites* at the time—a lesson that would be reinforced by my subsequent decade of tubby loneliness in our waif-worshipping monoculture—was that some women are flawless and tiny-boned like porcelain nightingales, and the rest of us are lonely, caustic basket cases in vintage dresses who make jokes to cover up our anxiety about having to go to the AIDS clinic. The nightingales get picked; we get settled for, if that.

Maybe that makes me sound stupid, but media is so strong. Media overpowers our conscious minds, no matter how hard we try to hang on—our knowledge of what is right, who has an agenda, what we are really worth. Marketing is powerful and beauty culture is powerful and men's control of the narrative is powerful and a lot of people are making a lot of money teaching us that we live in an unshakable natural hierarchy that bestows peace only upon those who achieve a narrow, subjective (and heavily monetized) version of perfection that just happens to look like white Barbie except less career oriented. I was on board. I was ready. Take my body, America.

Growing up, I didn't chafe at the shallow, exploitative representations of my gender I saw on-screen; I took notes. I added page after page to my mental list of how to be a woman and what I should yearn for (any attention, good or bad) and tolerate (anything short of violence, though it seemed a bracing slap was normal now and then) from men.

From makeover shows I learned that I was ugly. From romantic comedies I learned that stalking means he loves you and persistence means he earned you, and also that I was ugly. From Disney movies I learned that if I made my waist small enough, a man or large hog-bear might marry me and let me sit quietly in his castle until death. From sitcoms I learned that it's a wife's job to be hot and a husband's job to be funny. From *The Smurfs* I learned that boys can have seventy-eight possible personalities and girls can have one, which is "high heels." From *The Breakfast Club* I learned that rage and degradation are the selling points of an alluring bad boy, not the red flags of an abuser (and the thing is I STILL WANT HIM). From pretty much all film and TV I learned that complicated women are "crazy" and complicated men are geniuses.

In *Revenge of the Nerds*, the heroes break into a sorority house and install a hidden camera in the bathroom, then sell naked photos of the women they victimized. Later, the head nerd tricks one of the same women into having sex with him (which we have a word for, I think?) by disguising himself as her boyfriend. It's funny! Anything is okay as long as it's a joke!

Remember on *Dawson's Creek* when everyone alternately slut-shamed Jen and bugged her to fuck them for six seasons *and then she died*?

Remember in *Weird Science* when some virgins were horny, so they just *made a woman*?

Remember Fat Monica? I need a separate therapist just to deal with Fat Monica.

Even my precious *Bill and Ted* made Joan of Arc do aerobics at the mall.

From a very young age I learned that women are vain, hollow, pretty things—a lark for men to chase in between doing the real work of the world, a prize that makes them whole again, that missing rib. Boys, I can only assume by their behavior, absorbed some version of the opposite, a call to boldness, a certain intoxicating entitlement to every good thing. And why not? We should all be so lucky.

Everything is a product of its time, and the whole point of progress is to make the future better than the present. People make mistakes, and people grow, and culture grows along with them. I'm not so naive or narcissistic as to think that the media of my youth was deliberately trying to poison me or that there's nothing of value in things that hurt me. This is an imperfect history, anyhow, because there were strong women all around me, too, on screen and off, but figuring out who you are is always a triangulation of what you know and what you see. I knew that I was not inferior, but I could also see how the world treated girls like me.

Two years after the fall of Harvey Weinstein, TV and film are still in the thick of an unprecedented sociopolitical reckoning, a microcosm of our ongoing and ever-more-literal national culture war. But to make that reckoning stick, we have to look ahead and ask ourselves what we want of this new Hollywood and look back to avoid repeating the past. Show business could very well help get us out of this mess, but not if we fail to examine how it helped get us into it.

Hollywood is both a perfect and a bizarre vanguard in the war for culture change. Perfect because its reach is so vast, its influence so potent; bizarre because television and movies are how a great many toxic ideas embed themselves inside us in the first place. No matter how much lip service we pay to equality and progress, how many mantras about loving ourselves and one another, how many inspirational memes we churn out to counteract the message, the basest culture—the culture that sells, the culture we're used to—is still there on-screen showing us how people are supposed to look and talk and fuck.

I know what the contestants on *The Bachelor* look like. *The Biggest Loser*, which tortures fat people for entertainment, ran for seventeen seasons and is being rebooted in 2020. In 2018, a spokesman for the Victoria's Secret Fashion Show said it doesn't feature trans or fat models because it's selling "a fantasy." I know that thin people, still, now and forever, would do anything not to look like me. Call it dieting or rebrand it "wellness," Oprah is still selling cauliflower pizza.

Do you know how noise-canceling headphones work? They have a built-in microphone that measures the ambient noise around you, then generates an inversion of that sound wave and adds it to the mix in your headphones. When a frequency meets its opposite—when the peaks of one mirror and coincide with the valleys of another—the result is called phase cancellation. The two waves cancel each other out. Silence.

What we really need from Hollywood is about a hundred years of phase cancellation.

We don't need neutrality; we don't need "nice." It's not enough to just stop being terrible. We need new work that actively challenges old assumptions, that offers radical models for how to conceive of ourselves and how to treat each other. We need artists and studios fighting for diversity because it's the right thing to do.

In the past few years, for the first time, we started talking in a large-scale, nonacademic way about the reality that sex in America isn't just an individualized act between two people, falling somewhere on the spectrum of sublime to criminal—it's the stuff corruption is made of, an atavistic shell game designed to maximize male pleasure and consolidate male power.

Unseating a couple (or a score or even a generation) of powerful abusers is a start, but it's not an end, unless we also radically change the power structure that selects their replacements and the shared values that remain even when the movement wanes.

And here's how you do it: *you do it.*

I have created only one television show, so I know that I am a rookie, but on my show, *Shrill*, we got to make all kinds of choices. We got to write the stories, we got to choose who the characters were, we got to choose who we cast, we got to hire the writers and the directors and the crew. We had studio and network input on each choice, of course, but we had a tremendous amount of power too. Whatever your sphere is, however big or small, you get to make choices within it, and if you care about healing the wounds of the world I hope you become a real demon bitch about diversity and never let anyone sleep. Think radical thoughts and let yourself imagine they're true. Then ask yourself why it's considered radical to make art that accurately reflects reality, to build a society that takes care of its members, to demand a better world.

That said, the kind of deep, revolutionary changes we need won't come just from individual creators making individual choices on individual projects. Demographics have to change all the way up to the top in order to unseat the past.

According to data compiled by 50/50 by 2020, a coalition of entertainment professionals fighting for intersectional equity in Hollywood, a staggering 94 percent of film executives are white, 96 percent of film directors are men, 76 percent of writers across all platforms are men, and 81 percent of board members in Hollywood are men. The 50/50 by 2020 manifesto reads, "Men have used patriarchy and white supremacy to create a reality that centers their own needs, normalizing our oppression. This must end." We can bring reality back to reality if we change who makes the choices.

Art didn't invent oppressive gender roles, racial stereotyping, or rape culture, but it reflects, polishes, and sells them back to us every moment of our waking lives. We make art and it makes us, simultaneously. Shouldn't it follow, then, that we can change ourselves by changing what we make?

The movement can't just disrupt the culture; it has to become the culture. Anything else is just a red herring.

Always Meet Your Heroes

I have recently developed a minor ailment, something of which I am not ashamed and yet do not broadcast to the public lest it change their opinion of me as an elegant tastemaker. But I do not believe in guilty pleasures, so here goes. I am obsessed with the Food Network original program *Guy's Grocery Games*, and I will watch as many consecutive episodes as the Food Network will feed me.

Guy Fieri does the same joke in every episode of *Guy's Grocery Games*. At the beginning of each round, when the cheftestants have just heard the kooky limitations of their next challenge (mandatory marshmallow fluff in their chicken-fried steak or a punishingly small grocery cart), they stand poised at the starting line, nervous, eager to be unleashed upon Flavortown Market. They cannot begin to shop and cook until Guy Fieri says the magic words that begin His games: "Three, two, one, GO!"

As the cheftestants have recently discovered—assuming that this is their first time on television—most of show business is waiting around while people with complicated belts move heavy things that you are not allowed to touch. Then, once every couple of hours, a lot happens, briefly. It doesn't take very long on a set to figure out that, no, we're not starting yet. Only dorks are rarin' to go. Here Fieri springs his trap.

Exploiting the cheftestants' faith in their newfound expertise—their certainty that *nothing is happening yet*—he looks down at his cards and up again, nonchalant, just making chitchat. He points his toe and draws a lazy figure eight on the linoleum. They are probably just waiting for the grip to fix something with the lights, the cheftestants figure, or maybe camera is unsatisfied. Maybe someone from electrical has diarrhea. "You know," Fieri might say in this moment, this uneasy limbo, "*Three* Dog Night is a great band." The cheftestants nod politely at the small talk; maybe one gamely joins in, "Yeah, so great!"

"I saw them *two* years ago at the Clearwater Casino," Fieri goes on.

A pause.

"But they didn't play '*One* (Is the Loneliest Number).'"

Another pause.

"I had to *go* ask for my money back."

The pause quickens. Fieri looks at the cheftestants expectantly. They look back. He looks. They look. They can tell he wants something from them, but what? Fieri's eyes begin to twinkle. This is the frisson he lives for.

This is his moment.

He turns to the judges and shrugs ostentatiously. Aarti Sequeira bites her fist and bounces a little in her seat; she yearns to spill the beans. Fieri turns and looks straight into the camera—every time, he does this—and says something like "Not so quick, are they?"

At last the cheftestants get it. The magic words! They were hidden in Fieri's anecdote about the seventies boogie rock group Three Dog Night! Their time! Their precious, already comically inadequate time!

As the cheftestants panic and scatter—tasked with the compound indignity of preparing a killer chicken parm in twenty minutes using only ingredients from odd-numbered aisles *while having just been pranked by a human flip-flop*—Fieri luxuriates in his deception. He chuckles to himself, he rolls his eyes to the ceiling. "Now they got it," he says. Those idiots.

Fieri does this literally every time. He never, not once, has ever said, "Three, two, one, GO!" in the normal fashion. Yet somehow it works every time. The cheftestants are fooled every time. Fieri cannot believe his own genius every time. I am obsessed.

Guy's Grocery Games is currently in its eighteenth season.

There are three possible explanations for the persistent effectiveness of the three-two-one-GO gag:

1. No cheftestant who appears on *Guy's Grocery Games* has ever watched an episode of *Guy's Grocery Games.*
2. The cheftestants are humoring Fieri as though he were a child they cannot bear to disappoint.
3. The bit is sanctioned and staged by the producers as a classic element of Triple G.

Obviously, number three is most likely. But I prefer to believe it's number two, that the world is good and kind, at least in Flavortown.

My favorite thing about Guy Fieri is that he is objectively terrible at talking about food and only says four things ("That's the real deal!" "You've got the salty from the pork, the sweet from the sauce, the crunchy from the lettuce, that's the real deal right there!" "Killer!" "This is Flavortown, baby."). Occasionally, he interacts with actual celebrity chefs—in, perhaps, a Triple G Blazin' Bitchin' All Starz Edition: Flame-Broiled or BUST, BAYBEE. One's heart leaps to one's throat. Will our boy be embarrassed? Will the chefs smirk and be cruel? Will they tell him that "amazeballs" is not a word or decline his humble offering of Donkey Sauce? But what happens is the opposite: A glowing kindness floods the studio. The chefs smile at Guy, they encourage him, they cheer him, they compete in his *Grocery Games* as though they were chasing Olympic gold. It is pure sweetness.

There is something irresistibly endearing about Guy Fieri, perhaps not in spite of his gaucherie as a broadcaster but because of it. Watching deeply competent colleagues humor and encourage this strange saxophone of a man as he bungles around like a golden retriever is medicine. It is okay to like this dog and his bungling. This is a difficult time, and it is okay to go to another place once in a while. Donald Trump is not the president of Flavortown.

But, and here I reach my point: as much as Triple-G is a balm for my soul, when that day comes that it is revealed that Guy Fieri owns a puppy mill or did 9/11, he will pass from my life like so many before him. This is the slow, dumb work of progress.

Chip and Joanna Gaines fix up houses. Chip, a strapping blond man who looks like he is named Chip, does the construction, and Joanna, one of those infuriating people who seems to be smart *and* funny *and* talented *and* pretty *and* nice, is in charge of design. The formula of their show *Fixer Upper*, which ran for five seasons on HGTV, was simple but foolproof: First, live in Waco, Texas, where 14,000-square-foot midcentury mansions somehow cost $74,000. Knock down all interior walls. Cover every surface in "shiplap," which is expensive for "boards." Add one wall clock the size of Jupiter's moon Callisto. Contract local youth pastor/blacksmith to create custom art piece spelling the family's last name out in reclaimed horseshoes. Repeat.

The big reason to love Chip and JoJo is for the banter. Regularly, throughout each episode, the action will pause and Chip and JoJo will address the camera about the trials and tribulations on the job site and at their home, which they share with their forty perfect children. They generate charming bloopers. They laugh and tease each other. Sometimes Chip will get a little hornay and honk JoJo's butt. They are keeping it tight and keeping the spice alive. They are, as the adults trying to sound like the kids say, #relationship #goals—the type of love that none of us deserves. They are ravenously beloved, by me as much as anyone.

Fixer Upper ended its run in 2018, not out of a lack of public interest in Chip and JoJo but the extravagant opposite. In addition to their brick-and-mortar store, Magnolia Market, they also have a print magazine, *The Magnolia Journal* ($7.99 an issue), and, a year after the end of *Fixer Upper*, the couple announced that they would be developing their own *entire television network*, the Magnolia Network. "The difference moving forward is Jo and I are going to be able to tell more of our life stories," Chip told *USA Today*. "And so, as opposed to it being a very narrow vein in our universe, which is obviously construction and design and the things we do for a living, for us we feel like there's a more holistic story to be told here, and that's what we're going to focus on."

The Magnolia Network is scheduled to debut in the summer of 2020, and based on my calculations of their professional trajectory, Chip and JoJo will be . . . *beep-boop-beep-beep-beep-boop-boop* . . . fully running the galaxy by 2028. Well, to be more specific, JoJo will be Glorious Milky Way Hegemon of Earth and Void, and Chip will be Intergalactic Minister of Dropping a Space Hammer on His Foot Because He Saw a Centipede.

But there was a perilous moment, in December 2016, when the prospect of a business venture dedicated to more of the Gaineses' universe might not have seemed like a wise business move. BuzzFeed published a story that very briefly threatened to upend the Gaines empire, to much handwringing in both the pro-Gaines and Gaines-critical camps.

BuzzFeed reported that the Gaineses were members of Antioch Community Church, a megachurch whose pastor, BuzzFeed said, described the HGTV stars as "dear friends." That same pastor, Jimmy Seibert, unfortunately for the Gaineses but more unfortunately for any gay children in his congregation, also disapproves of marriage equality and believes that conversion therapy is a good and reasonable thing to do to LGBTQ children.

I assume it goes without saying among the readers of this book, but you cannot "convert" people from the essence of their being, and even if you could, you should not, and even if being gay or trans *wasn't* the essence of a person's being, you still should just let that person fucking live how they want to, and the way that many religious organizations do try to "convert" gay kids to being straight is cruel, traumatizing, and painful. Sam Brinton, the director of advocacy at the Trevor Project, a suicide prevention organization for LGBTQ youth, has written about surviving conversion therapy. Brinton, who is gender fluid and uses they/them pronouns, endured a counselor saying that Brinton was an abomination who would get HIV and AIDS. The torture was physical, too:

> The therapist ordered me bound to a table to have ice, heat, and electricity applied to my body. I was forced to watch clips on a television of gay men holding hands, hugging, and having sex. I was supposed to associate those images with the pain I was feeling to once and for all turn into a straight boy.

That kind of treatment—still legal in forty-one American states in 2019!—is what Chip and JoJo's spiritual leader believes in. The American Medical Association, the American Psychological Association, and the American Academy of Pediatrics all call it harmful. According to the BuzzFeed report, in a sermon after the Supreme Court legalized same-sex marriage in 2015, Seibert preached:

> We *can* change, contrary to what you hear. I've worked with people for over 30 years—I have seen hundreds of people personally change their direc-

> tion of same-sex attraction from a homosexual lifestyle to a heterosexual lifestyle. It doesn't mean they don't struggle with feelings, it doesn't mean that they aren't hurting, it doesn't mean it's not challenging. But they have chosen to change. And there has always been grace there for those who choose that.

Okay, buddy.

Defenders of Chip and JoJo were fierce in their outrage. How dare BuzzFeed pry into the private lives of such cheery and deadly charismatic celebrities? What about freedom of religion? How is their religious practice any of anyone's business, and how do we even know they agree with the church's stance on conversion therapy?

Twitter was aflame. The *Washington Post* ran an op-ed titled "BuzzFeed's Hit Piece on Chip and Joanna Gaines Is Dangerous" (witch hunt!), which argued that attending a homophobic church is fine because lots of people in the United States are homophobic.

Pastor Seibert, for his part, responded to the controversy in an audio interview with Tony fucking Perkins, of all people, surely to the pure delight and nothing-remotely-approaching-an-aneurysm of Chip and JoJo's PR team. Perkins, a truly evil quack, is the longtime president of the anti-LGBTQ extremist organization the Family Research Council, who relentlessly pushes the false claim that gay men are more likely to abuse children (pedophilia is "a homosexual problem," he says), insists that gay rights activism will lead to violence against Christians, and lobbied doggedly against antibullying policies implemented *after a spate of LGBT teen suicides.* A cool and totally normal guy! I'm sure we all have dear friends of dear friends who say things like this jewel from Perkins's close associate, the Executive Vice President of the Family Research Council: "[Islam] should not be protected under the First Amendment, particularly given that those following the dictates of the Quran are under an obligation to destroy our Constitution and replace it with sharia law."

Thousands of people attend Antioch Church in Waco. It is a megachurch. We have no information as to how often Chip and Joanna actually attend, how seriously they adhere to Antioch's tenets, what they might have found personally healing or comforting in that spiritual community, whether they actually consider Seibert a "dear friend" or if he was just blowing smoke up his own ass. Two congregants cannot reasonably be expected to repair every moral flaw in their church's entrenched culture, and it is, perhaps, a slippery slope to consider an HGTV celebrity tainted by way of which virulent bigot to whom their pastor chooses to grant his first post-homophobia-scandal interview. It is certainly arguable that that's a degree of separation too far. But man, it just sucks. And we should be able to say it sucks without histrionic op-eds calling us "dangerous."

Eventually Chip addressed the controversy himself, writing (rather noncommittally):

> Joanna and I have personal convictions. One of them is this: we care about you for the simple fact that you are a person, our neighbor on planet earth. It's not about what color your skin is, how much money you have in the bank, your political affiliation, sexual orientation, gender, nationality or faith. . . .
>
> We are not about to get in the nasty business of throwing stones at each other—don't ask us to cause we won't play that way.

Come on, man, just disavow that shit! You're killing us! We love the banter and the buns honking! Do it for the banter, or MAYBE DO IT FOR THE LGBTQ YOUTH SUICIDE RATES.

Observant viewers pointed out that—despite Chip's assertions that he and his wife don't throw stones at all human beings equally—*Fixer Upper* had not featured a single gay couple in its four seasons on the air, a rarity on an extremely gay network. The show fixed that omission in season five.

Two days after the BuzzFeed story was published, HGTV released the following statement: "We don't discriminate against members of the LGBT community in any of our shows. HGTV is proud to have a crystal clear, consistent record of including people from all walks of life in its series."

And it worked. The controversy died away. For the general public, that torture-gay-people-until-they're-straight bombshell did not stick, and—in the usual way of things—will instead impact only *Fixer Upper*'s LGBTQ fans and their allies, who now have to think about conversion therapy every time they want to watch the (maybe) deserving citizens of Waco, Texas, obtain slightly nicer sconces.

There's an insidious meme format that's been circulating regularly since the 2016 election. It's usually a photo of two white people standing, smiling, next to a barbecue grill. Maybe they are wearing sports memorabilia from the same team. Maybe they are sharing Thanksgiving leftovers. The caption usually reads something like "This is Donk. He's my neighbor. He voted for Trump. I voted for Hillary! That doesn't stop us from watching the big game together on the game day! Nachos and darts! CONNECTION, not DIVISION, is what is going to save this country!!!!!!!! [AMERICAN FLAG EMOJI BICEPS EMOJI, HEART EMOJI, ONE BIG EYE ONE SMALL EYE DIAGONAL TONGUE EMOJI]."

Now, it is true that it is good, potentially, to know and respectfully share ideas across cultural and political borders. It is not illegal to have bad, even evil, ideas, nor should it be. But there's a reason why these memes are almost always made by white people about white people. It is not good or healing or compulsory for marginalized people to connect with those who disagree that they should get to be full human beings under the law. Not everyone has the luxury of detaching from politics for an afternoon to eat a hot dog. And yes, I know this is complicated. I love Chip and JoJo, too.

Inevitably, in any critical analysis of pop culture like this, there comes a point when one party throws up his or her hands and asks, Why aren't we allowed to just have fun sometimes? Whatever happened to escapism? It's just a TV show! Let the people have the TV show!

And look, I am an escapism queen. I love to have the TV show. But what good is a vacation if certain people are dehumanized and tortured there? That's going to be a ZERO STARS from me, dog!

Sidestepping reality—whether you genuinely believe in, say, conversion therapy or just don't want to deal with some bullshit your pastor got you into—is choosing the lie. This is what I'll never understand about that tactic: people are *dying* to forgive you if you just live in the truth.

Since the 2016 election, conservative celebrities have been complaining that their political views make them unpopular in Hollywood. "Hollywood Conservatives Say

More Stars Stay Quiet to Avoid Public Backlash, Being Blacklisted," read a Fox News headline in 2018. "There used to be more of us," eighty-four-year-old Pat Boone told *The Hollywood Reporter.* "Tom Selleck, Jon Voight, Bruce Willis, who were outspoken, but they've been browbeaten and ridiculed, which is the main instrument on the left to shut us up." James Woods is forever whining on Twitter. Tim Allen says that doing comedy right now "is like dancing on the thinnest ice."

Well, good! I'm glad this is uncomfortable for you! The partisan divide is not insignificant or cute. Children are dying in ICE custody. In May 2019, twenty-three-year-old Muhlaysia Booker was killed in Dallas (just a ninety-minute drive from Waco), the fifth black trans woman to be murdered that year. It is not, as Chip wrote, "throwing stones at each other" to point out that these things are incompatible with basic morality. There is value in understanding those who disagree with you—some of us want to go wild on the backsplash with a pop of Moroccan tile, and some of us are white subway tile to the bone—but we're not living in a meme. There is no value in willfully ignoring hatred, and the lie that neutrality in the face of oppression is not a political stance is part of how we got here.

People are not binary. We are not good or bad, saintly or irredeemable. There's nothing wrong in asking for accountability and an acknowledgment of shared humanity from the people we admire, the people building the culture our children will grow up in, the people to whom we give our money. Who doesn't want to be better? What—you want to stay bad or get worse out of spite?

Every person is, to varying degrees, a fixer upper (SORRY*). Go salvage some shiplap.

* JUST KIDDING I'M NOT SORRY AT ALL SUBMIT THIS SENTENCE TO THE PULITZER COMMITTEE.

Do, Make, Be, Barf

Culver City, Los Angeles, was socked in by haze, and a line of women in black athleisure—more blondes than one is accustomed to seeing in one place at one time—stretched down the block. Each of us had paid between $500 and $1,500 to stand in this line and attend In Goop Health: Presented by Goop, the inaugural "health and wellness expo" of Gwyneth Paltrow's lifestyle brand, Goop.

Paltrow launched Goop as a sort of new-agey newsletter in 2008 and by 2018 had grown the company into a website, a store, a print magazine, a podcast, a Netflix series, and, most important, a brand, all together valued at $250 million. The brand, essentially, is Gwyneth herself—the implicit promise that commerce can transform toads into princesses, that enough kale and Manuka honey can turn my sweaty, dumpy ass into a willow tree. I went to Culver City that hazy day in 2017 to find out.

People were excited, a little nervous and giddy. It felt as if we were waiting for the bus to summer camp, if your summer camp gave out free lube and Nicole Richie was there. At 9:00 a.m., the beefy security team parted and we poured into a courtyard where employees sorted us based on how much we had paid to be there. Color-coded bracelets indicated whether you were a Lapis ($500), Amethyst ($1,000), or Clear Quartz ($1,500) Gooper. More money meant more activities: a foam roller workout, a "sound bath," even lunch with "GP" herself in the "Collagen Garden." A prohibitively expensive, celebrity-studded self-help salon wasn't exclusive enough; apparently the very rich can't have fun without a little class hierarchy.

We passed into a second courtyard, which offered clusters of tasteful white furniture ringed by a variety of "wellness adventures." In one corner, you could sit cross-legged on a cushion and the "resident Goop shaman" would tell you which crystal you "need." In the opposite corner was a woman who would photograph your aura in a little tent. There was an oxygen bar. There was an IV drip station. And there was food, of course, just in very small pieces: tiny vegan doughnuts, quinoa and lox swaddled in seaweed, ladles of unsalted bone broth, fruit.

I took a lap around the courtyard and the cavernous hangar where I would be spending the next nine hours (there was no reentry). Inside, interspersed among the Goop-approved matcha and coconut water stalls, was the Goop Marketplace, where attendees could buy face potions, rolling pins, and Tory Burch's new line of activewear. For $55, you could buy one of the jade eggs that Goop famously suggested women carry around in their vaginas. Or a rose quartz egg, if you had "seen results with the jade egg and want to take your practice a step further." I headed back outside and got in line for the shaman.

Turned out, the shaman was a little backed up, so they were scheduling appointments instead. A friendly employee wrote my name on a clipboard and told me to come back at 4:05 p.m. The line for aura photography was even longer. I waited about ten minutes before a staffer announced that the schedule was full and we were all fired from the line, but we could check back later. That was fine. Everyone was feeling good. Employees wove through the crowd with trays of probiotic juice. I decided I liked the Goop expo. It was silly, but most of us seemed to be in on the joke—like Dungeons and Dragons for your vaginal flora. Why not make life a little more magical by believing in magic? What's the harm?

In Goop Health was not my first foray into the Goop life. When I wrote for Jezebel, I frequently covered (made fun of) Paltrow's evolution from movie star to lifestyle guru. As part of my research (being a dick), in 2014, I purchased a copy of her diet book *It's All Good: Delicious, Easy Recipes That Will Make You Look Good and Feel Great* and set out to test her promise on myself. What if I spent a week eating only Gwyneth-approved twigs and barleys? Would I look good? *Would I feel great?*

The questions I sought to answer during one week in June 2014 were:

1. Did Gwyneth Paltrow really deserve all the shit I had given her for believing that water has feelings and that duck bacon is a "pantry staple"?
2. Was eating vegan and gluten free really the "detoxifying" miracle cure she made it out to be?
3. Could I even *do* it?
4. What the fuck are toxins?

And 5. Most important, by the end of the week, *would I be more ethereal*?

The answers to those questions, in order, were: yes, no, kind of, who fucking knows?, and [floats away on a gossamer wisp].

Turned out I could do it, but poorly. My Goop food diary went something like this:

I spent $300 on three days' worth of groceries.
Not my fault, really, but JESUS.

I almost barfed up my wet almonds.
For my morning snack on the first day, I was supposed

to eat "a handful of Soaked Raw Almonds." Soaking the almonds is very important, says Paltrow:

> Almonds have an enzyme in their coating that makes them difficult to digest. The harder anything is to digest, the more work your body has to do to get to all the nutrients and the more you miss out. Good news though! If you simply soak raw almonds in plenty of water for at least half a day, the enzyme will break down and you're good to go.

Something about those almonds was odious to me. I chewed and chewed, but they never seemed to go anywhere—they just circulated around my mouth, breaking into smaller and smaller chunks of nut-flavored eraser. I hated them. The wet almonds kicked off a faint, latent nausea that lingered for the entire week.

I exploded the blender.

Lunch one day called for "Beet Greens Soup." I didn't read the recipe all the way through, so I didn't realize until the soup was almost done that it was a *blended* soup.

I knew that you aren't supposed to blend boiling hot liquids, but it was 2:00 p.m., and all I'd eaten that day was kale juice and erasers. I had to risk it. I poured half the soup into the blender and started slow. A few pulses. Everything seemed fine. I was emboldened. "Liquefy."

I dumped soup all over the floor.

"It's okay," I reasoned. "I'll just pour the half-blended soup back into the pot and call it 'Semi-Blended Beet Greens Soup.' It'll be good. It's *all good.*"

I twisted the blender to disengage it. Instead of coming off intact, the glass pitcher unscrewed from its base, sending soup gooshing out the bottom. I screwed it back tight as fast as I could. There was soup in my shoe. I was so hungry.

I dropped the blender onto my foot.

"FINE. I'll just pick up the whole thing and pour it back into the pot with the base attached."

The base fell off. Onto my foot. I cried.

The soup hot pink leaf water was actually pretty good.

I set the chicken on fire.

I was basically delirious by the time dinner ("Barbecued Chicken, Spanish Style") rolled around. The rub smelled so good I could have eaten the chicken raw. Gwyneth didn't even tell me to take the skin off! I threw it on the grill, closed the lid, and turned the heat "down."

Five minutes later, my then boyfriend, now husband broke the news to me: "Baby, the chicken's gone." I teared up and asked him what he meant.

"You set it on fire. You must have turned the heat up instead of down."

I was genuinely sobbing at that point. "Is any of it edible? Is it at least cooked all the way through?"

"I have no idea," he said, laughing. "I don't know how long you're supposed to cook chicken at a million degrees."

I never got around to making the asparagus.

I was going to be late for Aqua Zumba. I had to shovel some semicremated, semiraw chicken down with my fingers and run.

I burned about a quarter of the roasted beets/butternut squash/shallots for my quinoa salad, a true tragedy because that was the best thing I ate all week.

Update: This recipe is so good, and I still make it.

I accurately followed Gwyneth's recipe for avocado smoothies.

Avocado, raw cacao powder, ground hemp seeds, almond milk, coconut water, raw honey. I couldn't find ground hemp seeds, even at the hippie grocery store, so I tried to pulverize them myself using a mortar and pestle. The result was chunky.

As I recall it, this mixture could give diarrhea an existential crisis. Gwyneth described the flavor as "beautiful."

I couldn't find a bass.

Me: "Excuse me, where's your bass?"

Brusque fishmonger: "NO BASS."

My salt was too big.

The salt I bought to bake my "[Not a Bass] Roasted in Salt, Thai Style" in turned out to be more like the kind of salt you use to deice a driveway. Inevitably, a few boulders found their way into each bite of fish, making it more like "Roasted Salt, Fish Style."

I hit a fish with a hammer.

Gwyneth Paltrow told me to break through the salt crust with a mallet, which it turns out is French for "fish exploder."

I injured my neck from too much chopping.

With the exception of the wet almonds and the shit shake, I have to say that every recipe I tried was actually great and to be perfectly honest this cookbook will rock your mouth and you should buy it. But in order to cook two full meals from scratch every day, I had to take *hours* out of the middle of my workday to chop, essentially, *one of every vegetable*, and then clean my entire kitchen three times a day. If I hadn't worked from home, had a flexible, non-physically-exhausting job, had the money to afford kitchen gadgets such as juicers and blenders, and had a supportive partner willing to run backup, I would have been shit out of luck. Not to mention the disposable income needed for groceries alone. This is a meal plan for people with a housekeeper and a chef. In other words, people with Clear Quartz bracelets.

The extremely problematic class implications of making wealth a prerequisite of "wellness" would come up exactly zero times at In Goop Health.

Now, I don't personally believe that my proximity to crystals (or lack thereof) has any effect on my well-being, but I don't think it is interesting or sophisticated to mock people who do. The women in the hangar and in line for the shaman with me were having fun. They were sitting on pillows and connecting with one another. They were having the kind of spontaneously intimate conversation that happens among women all the time, dressed up in the language of magic and, sure, monetized.

Maybe some of those were even the roots of the kinds of conversations we so desperately need to have: Oh, that happened to you? Me too.

As long as you are not promising miracles and swapping carnelian for childhood vaccines, organizing your inner life around crystals doesn't seem that much different from organizing it around Fitbits or "bullet journaling." There is a line, of course, between having fun with rocks and exploiting people's fears for profit, and I approached that line soon enough.

A few hours into my Goop fest lock-in, I looked up and there she was, gliding through the Bulletproof Coffee line like our priestess. Here is just a true fact: Gwyneth Paltrow glows like a radioactive swan. She emits light. She would be great in a power outage.

Though the FAQ for In Goop Health specifically directed attendees to wear athleisure (with a link to the Goop store's athleisure page—just to be helpful!), Paltrow appeared to be wearing a sirocco of flower petals. She led us, her flock, into the auditorium, and the real show began.

After a brief history of Goop ("I started to wonder: Why do we all not feel well? Why is there so much cancer? Why are we all so tired?"), Paltrow introduced her personal physician, Dr. Habib Sadeghi. He spoke for an hour about "cosmic flow"; his left testicle; the "magnificence" of Paltrow ("I've been down and I've touched her feet . . . and I'll do it again"); and his belief that "consciousness precedes phenotypic expression," which means, I guess, that all ailments are on some level psychosomatic and your ovarian cysts are really just little nodules of emotion.

The next panel, on gut health, countered Sadeghi's consciousness theory with the assertion that all human illnesses are actually caused by antibiotics, ibuprofen, cesarean sections, and legumes. The human gut is a rich rain forest, the panel members told us. Antibiotics are "napalm," and taking one ibuprofen is "like swallowing a hand grenade." Someone related an anecdote about a marathon runner who had to get a fecal transplant from her fat niece, and, tragically, it made the marathon runner fat. In mice, fecal transplants have been found to make fat mice thin and anxious mice calm. Oh, my God, I remember thinking. That's the final phase of Goop. Gwyneth is going to start selling her own shit.

Dr. Steven Gundry, the author of *The Plant Paradox*, revealed that from January to June, he consumes all his calories between 6:00 and 8:00 p.m., because "we evolved to search for food all day and then fast." It's funny how our understanding of human evolution—of the point at which we were once our truest selves—can shift according to which restrictive diet is on trend that day. Next to each of our chairs was a complimentary bottle of hot pink, watermelon-flavored water, sickly sweet with stevia. You know, just like the cavemen used to drink.

Gundry argued that human beings weren't meant to eat any plants native to North America, because we are native to "Africa, Europe, and Asia." (Just Africa, Steve! Just Africa!) At one point, a physician named Amy Myers casually distinguished between the gut bacteria Asian people need (because "they" eat a lot of seaweed) and the gut bacteria that "we" need. You didn't need to glance around the room to know who "we" was referring to.

In Goop Health was shockingly white—even to me, a blond white person who had gone in expecting whiteness. Obviously, this is anecdotal—I didn't conduct a postfest census—but I don't recall seeing more than ten people of color among the hundreds of attendees, and that's a generous estimate. The panelists were almost exclusively white.

I did wonder if anyone at Goop had brought up the lack of diversity in their speakers during the planning stages. But to acknowledge it would be to acknowledge politics, and In Goop Health stayed as far away from politics as it could get.

However, an event supposedly focused "on being and achieving the optimal versions of ourselves," as Paltrow put it during her welcome address, cannot truly be depoliticized. You can't honestly address "wellness"—the things people need to be well—without addressing poverty and systemic racism, disability access and affordable health care, paid family leave and food insecurity, contraception and abortion, sex work and the war against drugs and mass incarceration. Unless, of course, you are talking only about the wellness of people whose lives are untouched by all of those forces. That is, the wellness of people who are disproportionately well already.

Toward the end of his speech, Sadeghi told a story about an epiphany he'd had in the anatomy lab. He said he had discovered that the first valve of the heart flows straight back into the heart: "Selfish little organ there! No, no, not selfish—self-honoring. Wooo! What a difference! I could never give anything to anybody—ask my beloved wife—until I take care of me. Until my needs are met. Right? Right? When you fly down, the first thing that they tell you is that before you put the mask on anybody else, put it on yourself."

I heard that idea repeated over and over again at the Goop conference: take care of yourself so you can take care of others. Put your mask on first. Hold space for yourself. Be entitled. Take. At a certain point, it began to feel less like self-care and more like rationalization. I didn't know anything about the personal lives of the women at In Goop Health—where they donated their money, what hardships they had endured, why they were drawn to this event—and every person I interacted with was smart and kind and self-aware. But it is self-evident and measurable that white people in the United States, in general, are assiduous about the first part of that equation (caring for ourselves) and less than attentive to the second (caring for others).

It is okay to love skin cream and crystals. It is normal and forgivable to be afraid of dying, afraid of cancer, afraid of losing your youth and beauty and the currency they confer. We have no other currency for women.

I understand why people spend their lives searching for that one magic supplement, that one bit of lore that will turn their "lifestyle" around and make them small and perfect and valuable forever. I also understand, especially at this moment in history, why people long to step outside politics for a day and eat kale-flavored ice cream (real, not satire, actually good) in a warehouse full of Galadriels. But the idea that anything is apolitical is an illusion accessible only to a very few. And the absolute least the Galadriel in chief ought to do is acknowledge that.

At 4:05 p.m., after many hours of wandering, listening, and not having my aura photographed, I dashed outside for my shaman appointment, only to be told they were running about an hour behind. "Should I come back in an hour?" I asked. "I mean, you could try," the woman said in a way that meant "No" or probably "Not with *that* bracelet."

For her keynote to close the day, Paltrow promised to dissect the complexities and woes of being a working mother with a panel of famous gal pals: Cameron Diaz, Tory Burch, Nicole Richie, and Miranda Kerr. How do they do it? How do they have it all?

The women delivered a bounty of platitudes about ambition, female friendship, self-care, their mothers, and sticking to one's "practice." They were charming and humble and, of course, beautiful. Richie was funny. But at no point did any of them say the words "I HAVE LOTS AND LOTS OF MONEY AND A STAFF." In the context of a conversation about the challenges facing working mothers, the omission was, frankly, bizarre. It is a basic responsibility of the privileged to refrain from taking credit for our own good fortune.

They might as well have been reading from Ivanka Trump's 2017 book, *Women Who Work*, a hot choice if you're seeking life advice from someone who is more a logo than a person, a scarecrow stuffed with branding, an heiress turned model turned multimillionaire's wife playacting as an authority on the challenges facing working women so that she could, at one time, sell more pastel sheath dresses.

In that book, Ivanka wrote, "My father has always said, if you love what you do, and work really, really hard, you will succeed."

Love and hard work. That's all it takes! That's all Ivanka ever had going for her. Just a big fat work ethic and a whole lotta love. Nothing else. No, sir. "This is a fundamental principle of creating and perpetuating a culture of success, and also a guiding light for me personally."

She went on to say, "I also believe that passion, combined with perseverance, is a great equalizer, more important than education or experience."

Ah, yes, passion, that great "equalizer"—the passion to manage an entire household staff, the passion to have been born with the right bracelet. It might seem small, this lie by omission, but its roots worm and wend all the way down to America's original sin, our fundamental delusion: the bootstrap ethos, the notion that the comfortable deserve their place, that capitalism is an opportunity for the exploited to prove themselves, that success is a proportional reflection of hard work, that the rich are rich because they are good and smart. This deliberate spackling over of structural inequality—the death of luck—is the only thing that gives Donald Trump any authority. Well, he must know what he's talking about. Look how many ties he has!

There was one moment from the Goop conference that I still think about now, years later. Near the end of the keynote, Kerr casually mentioned that she had once tried leech therapy as part of her wellness practice. "One was on my coccyx because it's really good to, like, detox the body, rejuvenate the body," she said. "I had a leech facial as well. And I kept the leeches. They're in my koi pond."

I am fat. I was the fattest person at the Goop expo.

Strangers regularly contact me to tell me that I'm unhealthy and I'm going to die. A sampler from my emails:

"Being obese is NOT OK. It is associated with many health risks including: diabetes, high blood pressure, cardiovascular disease, and premature death. Go lose some weight you fat slob, and do it before you go on disability so we don't have to pay for you."

"I don't know what sort of message you are trying to send out to young girls/women, but that it is OK to be obese, and it is some sort of feminist sin to want to keep to a natural healthy shape can't be a good one."

Kerr's body is almost certainly what those people mean when they say "a natural healthy shape," because our society conflates conventional beauty with health.

But I don't know—I might be fat, but I've never felt as though I needed to get an IV drip on a patio in Culver City or put leeches on my butt to suck out toxins, and I'm grateful for that.

I guess Goop did make me feel well after all.

A Giant Douche Is a Good Thing if You're a Giant[*]

Did you know that *South Park* is *still on*? *South Park* came out when I was a freshman in high school, and it was *very outrageous* for the day, what with the anal probing of children and forcing Scott Tenorman to eat his own parents and things. My mother-in-law is a wild, wild lady, and when my husband was growing up, their house was a rule-free 25/7 indoor water balloon fight, but one directive never wavered: he was NOT ALLOWED TO WATCH *SOUTH PARK*. They did own a battered VHS tape of David Cronenberg's body horror classic "*Videodrome*," and *that* was fair game—James Woods ripping a ragged vulva in his alt-right abs was primo grade school content, but a racist ten-year-old farting fire was too far, too much,

* Yeah, yeah, yeah, yeah, yeah, yeah, yeah, yeah, yeah, yeah, yeah, yeah, yeah, yeah, yeah, yeah, yeah, yeah, I know that douching is actually not good. Let me have this.

too soon. That's how freaked out our parents were by that cartoon. In the 1990s, *South Park* was BY BAD BOYS FOR BAD BOYS.

When *South Park* premiered, creators Trey Parker and Matt Stone were naughty young twentysomethings on the edge, and I was in my last year of trick-or-treating. Of course it seemed dangerously spicy! Bad boys too bad for good girls! But now, in 2019, I am thirty-seven human years old—truly a kind of old person!—which makes Matt and Trey bona fide *full old*. These are dads, you guys. White millionaire dads! So isn't it a little strange that we still treat *South Park* like the daring vanguard of counterculture, when its creators, at this point, have more in common with Mitt Romney than [the coolest young person of whatever month you're reading this]? And, even more significantly, that their ideology appears not to have perceptibly shifted in the intervening twenty years, which means that *the Mitt Romney was coming from inside the house all along*? It was always there. We just gave them the benefit of the doubt because white men get to be their own mythmakers.

For decades—hahaha twenty-two seasons!—Matt and Trey have been telling us that they alone are the Reasonable Men, they alone stand against the indoctrination of both Right and Left, they alone know the truth, and the truth is that "both sides" are equally stupid, equally worthy of mockery, so the only rational response to any political argument is to snicker. And what is our mechanism, as an audience, for questioning that narrative, when *South Park* has been just as relentless in its insistence that criticism is censorship, that if you disagree with any of the show's choices you must be a moral scold, a damp-handed weepy little bitch, a boring person? It is so, so frightening, especially when you are young, to seem uncool. Taking a side against anything that happens on *South Park* would mean taking a side, and, as we've learned, both sides are equally stupid. The only safe space is nihilism.

It's a neat trap, which certainly does not sound like indoctrination at all.

But.

My friends.

Both sides, inasmuch as there are two "sides," are not equally stupid or equally bad. The notion that they are is human-extinction-level dangerous.

Maybe it took you until Donald Trump started tearing children from their parents and then LOSING THEM like he's fucking Andy Capp looking for his keys to notice that Republicans have slightly different priorities than even fully starfished, middle-of-the-bed centrist Democrats, and that's fine. We are all in process. But at this point, when we have maybe thirty more years (if we're lucky) before there *is no more ice* and many people on the right are over here calling for a RETURN TO MOTHERFUCKING COAL, and you're still smirking at the libs for being try-hard, bleeding-heart "social justice warriors" because we want our grandchildren to experience, I don't know, *fish*, then you have crossed the threshold from kicky contrarian into fully detached-from-reality genocidal psychopath.

In 2018, the People for the American Way—a liberal advocacy group founded by Norman Lear to counteract Jerry Falwell's Moral Majority—gave Matt Stone and Trey Parker something called the "Freedom Award" for doing freedom very good. Larry Elder, the libertarian-turned-big-R-Republican commentator who introduced them before they received the award (I don't fucking know why he was there), wrote on Twitter, "After they graciously accepted, they said, 'We're republicans.' Nervous laughter. They repeated, 'No, seriously, we're republicans.' #Priceless"

#Priceless!

Yes, it *is* hilarious that during perhaps the most hyper-partisan moment in modern history, when the Republican Party has shown itself to be the servile, invertebrate lapdogs of fascism, and the current Republican president has been accused of sexual assault by at least twenty-two women and is busy stacking the lower courts with barely disguised quasi-Nazi goons, a group of left-wing donors who came together to raise large sums of money in support of progressive causes such as (per the "campaigns" section of People for the American Way's website) "promoting gender equity" and "protecting lower courts" were confused when the men they were honoring in the name of "freedom" announced that, *actually*, they back the party of Grabbing 'Em by the Pussy.

How embarrassing that the vast swath of real estate between the Left and the Right—which grows wider all the time—actually has meaning to some people! How dare the stuffy scolds of the gala class silence these freedom fighters with their fearsome, censorious *checks notes* "nervous laughter"!

The implication, as usual, is that Stone and Parker aren't your daddy's Republicans, they're *cool guys*. They even tried to be good, nice Democrats—because they're *cool*, they're not racist or sexist or whatever—but liberal overreach, PC censorship, and lefty carelording finally became too much for these boys of freedom and they were exiled to the right, welcomed into the bosoms of the other Reasonable Men. MUCH LIKE AMERICA ITSELF.

When Stone and Parker made that "announcement" in 2018, the alt-right cheered that the libs had been officially owned. The Left harrumphed that those silly goofs must be doing a satire. But it wasn't really news. Parker and Stone have been calling themselves Republicans in public, over and over, since at least December 2001. That was when the pair got their first award from People for the American Way.

John Tierney, writing in the *New York Times* in 2006, recalled the event: "The audience, warmed up by an evening of lefty rhetoric, was startled to hear Stone and Parker announce they were Republicans."

They could have said libertarians, which are Republicans with sunglasses, but they said Republicans, specifically. "I hate conservatives," Tierney quoted Stone as saying, "but I really hate liberals." That, again, was 2001, when George W. Bush had just gone to war in Afghanistan—a war that, along with its fraudulent, for-profit spin-off, Iraq—would spend the next several decades forcing the children of impoverished Americans to massacre the children of impoverished brown people overseas. At the time, in those months after 9/11, Bush had his highest approval rating ever, which is perhaps why the American public (which was hyperpartisan even then, don't you remember?) didn't bat an eye at their snotty cartoon counterculture heroes self-identifying as Dwight D. Eisenhower superstans. But in retrospect, is there a worse time in history to proudly call yourself a Republican? (2016: "Hold my beer."*)

This mental contortion came to be called "*South Park* Republicanism," an ideology that we can easily recognize now as a sort of proto-alt-right—predominantly young white men who felt "bullied" by un-fun, po-faced liberals and chose to fight back not with vicious stereotyping

* I apologize for how hack "Hold my beer" is even at the time of this writing, but it conveys a specific idea with great efficiency and the slang gods have not yet come up with an alternative. I am hoping that it will come back around, like "Wazzzaaaaaap."

and oppressive social programs like their GOP dads had done but with vicious stereotyping and *irreverence* (and tacit endorsement of oppressive social programs).

In 2004, asked about their politics again, Parker and Stone clarified:

> Basically, if you think Michael Moore's full of shit, then you are a super-Christian right-wing whatever. And we're both just pretty middle-ground guys. We find just as many things to rip on on the left as we do on the right. People on the far left and the far right are the same exact person to us.

I just want to take a moment to make one thing clear, to shine a spotlight on this one specific idea: *It is very important that people not feel this way.*

Liberals are imperfect. Yes, of course. Liberals need to grow one fucking vertebrae, stop massaging capitalism's nards, and actually serve their constituents. But, on the other hand, if you look at the actual fucking laws they are trying to pass and the actual fucking leader they are supporting, the Republicans of 2019 literally do not want human beings to have health care. They do not want millennials to be able to earn a living wage, own property, or comfortably retire, ever. They want to expand access to guns and shrink police accountability. They want refugees tossed into concentration camps. They want pregnant people to be forced to incubate and birth unwanted children and for barely pubescent rape victims to die in childbirth. They certainly want to roll back marriage equality, if they can, and they've already begun stripping rights and protections from trans people. They want to squeeze every last resource out of our ecosystem until everything you love—manatees, dragonflies, fruit, your grandchildren—either burns or starves or drowns. They want to steal your money and waste it on gold-leafed steaks that they can shit into their gold toilets while they watch the sun swallow the earth. They are very, very bad! Similarly, sometimes Democrats ask you to respect people's pronouns!

The Trump era has produced an insidious strain of political amnesia, leading otherwise rational left-wing people to feel warm things for George W. Bush because he paints pictures of kitties and shares his gumdrops with Michelle Obama and because a toilet demon is president now and a bungling, babbling warmonger seems like a gorgeous statesman by comparison. (Sheepish disclosure: I briefly fell for the cat paintings.) But how can we forget so much so quickly? My parents literally had toilet paper with George W. Bush's face on it. Don't you remember how you felt before you knew that things could get worse?

Republicans were bad before Trump, and they will still be bad when he is gone. It is objectively destructive to fetishize the past, to dismantle social safety nets, to deny the existence of structural inequalities and leave the most vulnerable to face impossible odds without succor. It is a fundamental betrayal of everything a society is for.

There is no cool version of conservatism, no ethically responsible version, no rational version ready to reclaim the tiller after Trump leaves office. The word itself betrays an inherent violence: to conserve is to avoid change, to embrace stasis, to freeze frame the now because the now is treating certain people very, very well. And those who aren't being treated well under the current system? Better not complain. Wouldn't want to annoy Matt and Trey. Remember: black men locked up for drug crimes and forced to do slave labor in for-profit prisons are the "exact same person" as the white millionaires profiting from the prisons!!!!!!!!!!!!

In the 2004 episode "Douche and Turd," South Park Elementary holds an election to choose a new mascot after PETA objects to their previous mascot, a cow. The boys, obviously, think this is stupid and write in prank candidates; Kyle's suggestion is a giant douche, while Cartman's is a turd sandwich. The joke soon grows into a genuine dispute, which in turn erupts into a hotly contentious and corrupt election. Stan announces that a giant douche and a turd sandwich are exactly the same, and he refuses to vote, after which he is chased by a gun-wielding "Vote or Die" mob led by Sean "P. Diddy" Combs and eventually exiled from the town.

The episode aired just before the 2004 election in which John Kerry, a kind of uninspiring boring guy, was defeated by the incumbent, George W. Bush, a war criminal. You sure got 'em, boys!

Yes, PETA sucks. A stopped clock and all that. But the *South Park* guys are not mad at PETA for the things that actually suck about PETA. They're mad at PETA for being annoying, for caring too hard about animals (however imperfectly). This is not some new, cool strain of conservatism—nor is the alt-right. This is the same old stuff. It's Morning in America. Make America Great Again. When I was a kid, "Save the whales" was a punch line, shorthand for those limp-wristed environmentalists, those tree people in their knitwear, always *caring* so *annoyingly* on your *doorstep* with their *clipboards.* Well, good news, jokers. We didn't save the whales. They're dying. Another victory for irreverence. Ha ha.

In researching this book I spent a few hours playing the *South Park* video game "South Park: The Fractured but Whole" on my PlayStation 4. In it, you play as the New Kid, joining a vast war of pretend superheroes that spans the entire town. It is possible that I just never got to the good parts, but I found it excruciatingly dull, a feat for a product striving so wildly to be edgy. (One minigame tasks the player with shitting in as many toilets as possible. Is there anything less controversial than something that comes out of *every butt on Earth*?)

The game piqued my interest when I was poking around for *South Park* background and came across this passage on Wikipedia: "The non-player character, PC Principal, can teach the player to recognize microaggressions, which allows the player a free in-battle attack against an enemy."

Perhaps nothing is more pathetic than a white millionaire dad sneering at the attempts of oppressed groups to articulate their daily grinding indignity and begging for that indignity to be seen. To take microaggressions—like, say, if you're a black gamer and a character in the video game you're playing (Cartman) names his superhero alter ego "The Coon" and invites you to his "Coon Lair" to teach you how to post photos to "Coonstagram" for extra points—and characterize them as a boon, a bonus, a life enhancement, a "free in-battle attack," instead of a hindrance? How fucking weak. Those bitches wouldn't last a day.

Twenty-two seasons since the inception of *South Park*, who doesn't remember the disabled kids in their class being called "Timmeh" and the black American kids being called "Token" and the Ethiopian immigrant kids being called "Starvin' Marvin," even though Ethiopia hasn't been in famine since the mid-eighties? That Ethiopian famine, the death toll of which some place at 1.2 million, displaced around 400,000 refugees—many of whom came to the United States and some of whom were thirteen when *South Park* debuted, blessed to spend the next twenty years being mocked for having watched their family and friends and neighbors die in a largely human-engineered catastrophe, which the BBC called "the closest thing to hell on Earth." Funny! Lighten up!

I understand that the whole point of *South Park* is to bait me into writing exactly this essay—into such self-serious "offense," but, sorry, if we let trolls dictate the parameters of what's right and what's wrong, what's acceptable and what's taboo, we end up with Donald Trump as president.

There's a meme that pops up a lot in social media arguments, toward the end, usually posted by whoever's arguing *against* PC snowflakes and *for* something extremely cool such as Louis CK making fun of the Parkland shooting survivors or Roseanne Barr comparing Valerie Jarrett to an ape. (I cannot confirm this, but it's not *impossible* that Ricky Gervais has this meme tattooed on the inside of his anus.) It is generally deployed as a mic drop, a weapon of mass rhetorical destruction, a big stinky nuke that no mortal could possibly withstand.

The meme goes like this: It's a photograph of the English comedian Stephen Fry, looking smug, beside the quote "It's now very common to hear people say, 'I'm rather offended by that,' as if that gives them certain rights. It's no more than a whine. It has no meaning, it has no purpose, it has no reason to be respected as a phrase. 'I'm offended by that.' Well, so fucking what?—Stephen Fry."

I mean, okay? I guess? The use of "offended" here—and, indeed, in all such discussions—is deliberately vague, much like the way the US media have been lured into using the obscure, ill-defined, not actually criminal term "collusion" to describe Donald Trump's activities instead of "felony fraud and obstruction of justice." *Of course* it doesn't matter if someone is "offended" if "offended" doesn't really mean anything. The implication is that "offense" is a dishonest, manipulative way to overstate "hurt feelings," an attempt to make a frailty of the offended into an aggression of the offender. And that is sometimes true—I occasionally get emails complaining about my use of profanity, for instance, an utterly fucking poopoo-brain complaint for doinks. But more often, "offended" indicates the inverse; it's a cloaking device intended to make large-scale, systemic social issues look smaller than they are, to turn class-based oppression into individual oversensitivity. Railing against the "offended" as a homogeneous group conflates two very different issues.

"Just a joke" is context dependent. Certain topics, such as rape, can be "just a joke" to some, but to others they require a degree of self-negation far beyond any reasonable cost-benefit analysis. So what exactly are Fry's parameters here? Is all "offense" equally unsympathetic, equally "whiny"? Is a Muslim person complaining about an Islamophobic joke the same as a golden retriever breeder who's "offended" because somebody said he doesn't like dogs?

Does the Muslim person's "offense" become more legitimate the closer its temporal proximity to a mass slaughter of Muslims by a white supremacist terrorist? Fry is gay; are gay people allowed to be "offended" by homophobia? Are gay people allowed to request respect and civility from their inner circle but not from their professional colleagues or the world at large? Or is any such request simply "whining"? If black people live in a country in which their community is so relentlessly stereotyped and flattened that they are regularly murdered by agents of the state and even the simple statement that their "lives matter" is met with frothing outrage from a heavily armed majority, is it "whiny" if they ask white people not to call them racial slurs? Are women—modern comedy's greatest bugaboo—justified in complaining about anything at all? What if, after years of being shouted down when they complained about lazy misogyny and rape apologia in comedy, women found out that several of the most rich and famous male comedians of all time were serial sexual harassers and rapists? Then do you think, Stephen, that those women's "offense" might be worth reexamination?

If by "gives them certain rights," Fry means "the right to demand basic human dignity" and "the right to offer critique about the world and one's place in it," I'm pretty sure we don't need the term "offended" to confer those. They are, respectively, innate and protected by the First Amendment (of which Fry-meme deployers are generally such fans!). And, anyway, Fry certainly seems offended by the term "offended," as though that gives him certain rights—why are we expected to respect that as a phrase?

Well, so fucking what?

There's a type of person who thinks he's getting away with something by not believing in anything. But not believing in anything *is* believing in something. It's active, not passive. To believe in nothing is to change nothing. It means you're endorsing the present, and the present is a horror. And why wouldn't a couple of straight white millionaire dads be invested in protecting the status quo? If they can do it under the guise of challenging the status quo, what better camouflage?

Irreverence is the ultimate luxury item.

Gear Swap

My husband plays the trumpet, which is a sort of loud pretzel originally invented to blow down the walls of fucking Jericho and, later, to let Civil War soldiers know it was time to kill each other in a river while you chilled eating pigeon in your officer's tent twenty miles away, yet somehow, in modern times, it has become socially acceptable to toot the bad cone *inside your house* before 10:00 a.m. because it's "your job" and your wife should "get up." What a world! If one was feeling uncharitable, one might describe the trumpet as a machine where you put in compressed air and divorce comes out, but despite this—despite operating a piece of biblical demolition equipment inside the home every bright, cold morning of his wife's one and only life—the trumpet is not the most annoying thing about my husband.

The most annoying thing about my husband, Ahamefule, is that he is obsessed with microphones. To be clear, this is also one of the most charming things about him, one of the things I love the most, because that's what love does to you—it scrambles your compass, so that the idiosyncrasies you hate with fire and fury become so fucking charming you just want to gobble that person up and then poop them into a baby's cradle and coo over them until the heavens fall into the sea. But that doesn't mean I don't know he's annoying! The thing is that Ahamefule doesn't just love microphones, he needs *me* to care about microphones, too. Sometimes, if I ask for a kiss good night, he won't give it to me until I can name the three types of microphone or answer a quiz question about acoustic foam. (Which I can't! We have not kissed in seven years.)

Ninety percent of the time, if I am talking about something important such as world hunger or myself, he is not listening because he's on Microphone Grindr thinking about getting matching towels that say HIS and HERTZ to share with a six-foot XLR cable, his real wife. (A case study: When I texted Ahamefule to get permission to make fun of his microphone addiction in this book so that we can send our children to college, he wrote back, "Of course. If you showed me a photo of you in a recording booth but your nose was replaced by a nutsack, I would definitely notice the type of microphone first." A pause. Then another text: "But you have to understand the significance of vibrations that occurred in the air at one point in time being preserved for all time. It is a miraculous human achievement." Pause. "It really is." Pause. "A microphone is one of the most beautiful things in the world.")

Ahamefule's favorite website is a Facebook page called Seattle Music Gear Swap and Sale, where long-haired rockmen sell one another recording equipment and tell stories about their favorite audio cables. Sounds pretty straightforward, right? I have a jazzy bass; you need a jazzy bass. I need an MXLR 700-Falcon Jabroni Pro 2C-4500XL-10 Analog Pre-Amp Monitor Phase Box: Platinum Limited IguanaDog6614 Black Ice Edition; you have an MXLR 700-Falcon Jabroni Pro 2C-4500XL-10 Analog Pre-Amp Monitor Phase Box: Platinum Limited IguanaDog6614 Black Ice Edition. Consider that gear swapped!

But in the past couple of years, a wicked (and not in the cool way that gear swappers usually use it!!!) rot has been devouring Seattle Music Gear Swap and Sale from the inside out, turning Daves against Mikes, Phils against Stans. That rot is called identity politics, cursed be its name.

First, though, a little background on the music business. A 2018 study by the USC Annenberg Inclusion Initiative analyzed six hundred songs that had appeared on the *Billboard* Hot 100 list from 2012 through 2017. Researchers found that not only did male recording artists outnumber female artists by a margin of 3.5 to 1, men make up 87.7 percent of songwriters and a staggering 98 percent of music producers. Out of 651 producers examined by the study, only two were women of color. Not 2 percent—*two people.*

Racial and gender disparities are just as pronounced among the technician class. According to census numbers analyzed by Data USA (an MIT-affiliated website that processes public government data into easily digested visuals), men make up 91.9 percent of broadcast and sound engineers, radio operators, and media and communication equipment workers. A full 78.6 percent of that workforce is white.

In the early 1990s, my now husband was living in Section 8 housing with his single mother, begging for a trumpet. He'd been drawn hungrily, inexorably, to music since he was a toddler, but a musical instrument—let alone private lessons—was a laughable expense for a family that didn't always have food. Miraculously, in the spring of his sixth-grade year, two important things happened on the very same day: a hard-up neighbor posted a flyer advertising a trumpet for sale, and my mother-in-law received her tax refund.

As soon as he was able to make music, Ahamefule was just as desperate to record it. His dream was to have some kind of multitrack recorder, but that wouldn't come until his midtwenties. Instead, he would tie a boom box with a built-in microphone to a string and hang it from the ceiling so he could record transcribed bebop solos and the originals he wrote for his grunge band, Cogito Glo (those recordings are lost to time, which is how I know we live in Hell). He read everything he could find about acoustics and frequencies and pieces of audio gear that cost more than his mom made in a year. To this day, he says, he remembers the placement of every microphone he's ever set up.

After middle school, Ahamefule enrolled at the rich, mostly white neighborhood high school and discovered that it offered audio engineering as an elective. Kismet, right!? There was clearly no one more deserving of taking audio engineering AT HIS PUBLIC SCHOOL than little audio savant freak Ahamefule J. Oluo, finally catching a break after a childhood of grinding poverty and disappointment, right? Sometimes the world is good!

One would assume at this point that little Ahamefule enrolled in the class and learned the basics of audio engineering and made connections with professionals in the field and got internships and mentorships and tips and tricks and references and maybe even hand-me-down equipment, setting him on the path to a steady, reliable career as a studio engineer and eventually perhaps even a record producer. Right?

NOPE. BECAUSE THAT SHIT COST $200. OR $40. HE DOESN'T REMEMBER. BUT $5 MIGHT AS WELL BE $50,000 IF YOU DON'T HAVE IT.

You might want to set this book down real quick and schedule a therapy appointment for five minutes from now, because the image of a little boy tearfully begging his mother for a relatively small amount of money so he can fulfill a lifelong dream of learning a skill at which he is preternaturally gifted *and her having to say no*, because she has nothing, while that same opportunity—again, an elective at a *public school*—is instead just handed out to any indifferent, rich shit looking for an easy A, IS A LOT FOR ONE HUMAN HEART TO PROCESS. Ahamefule did not come up with the money, and he did not get to take the class, and he did not become an audio engineer, and that's just the outhouse of a country that we live in.

That, again, was in the 1990s, when it was still somewhat feasible to live in Seattle on a working-class salary. Things have changed. The *Seattle Times* reported in 2018 that the median net worth of white Seattleites is $456,000. The median net worth of black Seattleites—and here you should probably *beep-boop-boop* that therapist again—is $23,000.

White net worth in my city is twenty times that of black net worth. If you are one of those people who believes that racism is a thing of the past, never existed at all, or is defined simply as one person being mean to another person, you are claiming that white people genuinely *earn*—through ability alone, because anything else would be a systemic advantage—twenty times as much as black people. White people are twenty times as good at their jobs, twenty times as skilled, twenty times as deserving. If you believe that, you are racist. That is racism. (Congratulations! I don't know if you've heard, but 2019 is a great time for you guys.)

Nationally, the median net worth of white families is a little more reasonable, *only ten times that of black families*. Ten fucking times! The *Washington Post* reported in 2017, "Nearly 1 in 5 black families have zero or negative net worth—twice the rate of white families." Being able to spend a few hundred bucks for a trumpet and more for an audio engineering class is the kind of investment that gives kids an early advantage, a foothold on a path beyond mere survival, but it's an investment that's wildly out of reach for many American families—and that disparity is absolutely racialized. These numbers reflect a pathologically racist society.

In the Annenberg study, despite obvious systemic inequalities of opportunity, 42 percent of artists were people of color. Despite everything (or perhaps because of it), American music is black music. The fact that a people who have a socioeconomic deficit of 1,000 percent still manage to dominate the American musical landscape (influentially, if not compensatorily) is a testament to what we are losing.

It was against that backdrop that Seattle Music Gear Swap and Sale saw the first stirrings of unrest.

I don't know where it started, but a few white male Gear Swap members—perhaps newly enwokened by Black Lives Matter or #MeToo, perhaps finally exorcising long-simmering guilt, perhaps just human men with basic mental processing skills and normal amounts of empathy—began offering minor discounts based on gender and race.

It was a simple, thoughtful, victimless gesture—intended to take the smallest chip, a grain of sand, out of the monumental walls of privilege and social conditioning and systemic disadvantage that funnel people down the same well-worn paths that determine which people are "the right fit" for which careers, who has the right experience, who's just a hobbyist versus who gets a good union job. Tackling something so basic as helping one person *afford the tools it takes to do something* (and charging for them! It's not even a handout!) is the gentlest of reparations, literally the least the privileged can do.

Naturally, upon seeing this, some of the white men of Gear Swap (#NotAllTheWhiteMenOfGearSwap) parkoured directly out of their fucking gourds. Individual sellers choosing to apply minor discounts to the sales of their own personal belongings as a small palliative for the glaring inequality and power imbalance endemic to their industry is tantamount to communism! AND fascism! AND MURDER. As every white reggae drummer knows, it is extremely sexist and racist to try and heal the ravages of sexism and racism. What if someone posted that his clarinet was for sale to WHITES ONLY or that her SM57 was $50 for real Americans and $7,000 for Muslims!? The libs would go wild!

I mean, for that matter, what if only 2 percent of producers on the *Billboard* Top 100 list were women, and what if black musicians were historically grifted out of their own profits and music rights by white executives!?!? Oh, wait.

Keith Richards likes to tell a story about the Rolling Stones' first trip to the United States in 1964: they visited Chicago's Chess Records and supposedly found blues legend Muddy Waters (whose 1950 hit "Rollin' Stone" had inspired the band's name and whose music they shamelessly plundered to stratospheric fame and profit) working as a handyman, painting the ceiling. That's a wild story, right? But the actual wildest part of that story is that it doesn't end with "And then we gave Muddy Waters a million fucking dollars!!!!!"

Now, a lot of people say that this story isn't even true. But it doesn't matter whether it's true or not, because it's Keith Richards telling it, and *even in his imagination* he doesn't give Muddy Waters a million dollars! GIVE FAKE MUDDY WATERS A PRETEND MILLION DOLLARS FOR STEALING THE BLUES FROM HIM, IMAGINARY PAST KEITH RICHARDS YOU RAGGEDY CORPSE.

Forgive me if I have minimal sympathy for a bunch of white dudes complaining about being charged a reasonable market price for equipment that they are going to use to make bad copies of music stolen from black people. (Notably, not one of them was complaining about the price of bagpipes.)

So this is the part where, in 99 percent of other non-social-justice-related internet forums moderated by middle-aged white guys, someone in charge would roll his eyes and take the path of least resistance, assuaging the legion of angry Geoffs by banning race- and gender-based discounts—case closed, political correctness foiled again.

Instead, a marvelous and singular thing happened at Seattle Music Gear Swap and Sale.

The two white moderators looked at the bloody scene before them, and they said (I'm paraphrasing) . . .

"People can sell their own shit for whatever they want. Stop bothering us with this."

!!!

!!!!!!!!

!!!!!

!

!!!!!!!!!!!!!!!!!!!!

And then here's the really important part—they just kept saying "Shut up, stop bothering us with this" to anyone complaining about the policy. Forever!

Yes, of course, the anti–identity politics people didn't go down without a fight, and yes, they got annoying, and they complained on every single post. And on every single post, every time, the moderators went in there and they didn't say, "Okay, fine," they said, "Oh, my God, you guys have to stop wasting our time with this stuff, we do not care what people want to sell their own belongings for, this page is for swapping and selling gear, so SHUT UP AND GET BACK TO SELLING AND SWAPPING GEAR OR LEAVE AND START YOUR OWN FUCKING GEAR SWAP." And every single time it was a miracle! And ban them they did! They banned people! And they kept banning people! And they kept defending the policy, and more and more people started offering the discounts, and on every discount post more aggrieved whites would complain, and then the moderators—with a delectable, escalating, red-hot exasperation—would tell them to shut up and then ban them.

As I said, I don't particularly care about gear. If anything, I view it as romantic competition. I am not a member of Gear Swap. I could not tell you what a preamp does, and I have logged probably seven hundred hours of conversation about them.

I tell you the Gear Swap story because I think it's instructive. You don't have to "hear both sides" perpetually—you can hear them once or twice, make a decision, and move on into the future. The Gear Swap mods made a decision and stuck to it and it worked. Their platform became stronger and more successful. It is a pleasant, civil, productive community.

Twitter could do this. Facebook could do this. In a more abstract way, our news media could do this. Our government could do this. All of them are desperate to keep you away from the truth: that they could make their platforms safe, constructive, and non-Nazi-infested for all users, but they *choose* not to.

The reasons for that choice are almost certainly dense and snarled: Social media platforms were largely built by men, who clearly did not anticipate the ways they could and would be weaponized against vulnerable users. It is devilishly difficult to retroactively fix a system that trolls have already figured out how to exploit. It is expensive to moderate all that content. On Twitter, the president of the United States generates towering traffic and publicity by using the platform as his brain toilet. On Facebook, bad actors spend money, too. Our national sociopolitical discourse is so hopelessly broken and partisan and foul that no one is starting from common ground. Right-wing propaganda has convinced even relatively intelligent people that we must "hear both sides" on moral no-brainers such as NAZIS = BAD. Left-wing gullibility, always seeking to do the right thing, falls for it every time.

And there is one other reason, perhaps. Men think that misogyny is a women's issue; women's to endure and women's to fix. White people think that racism is a pet issue for people of color; not like the pure, economic grievances of the white working class. Rape is a rape victim's problem: What was she wearing? Where was she walking? Had she had sex before?

That's like if your doctor botched your bunion surgery and amputated both your feet and you went back to complain and the doctor said, "Don't look at me! I have both my feet!"

In 2013, in the stylish atrium of a Seattle ad agency, I moderated a panel for the 3 Percent Movement, an organization founded to address the dismal statistic that at the time of its beginnings, only 3 percent of advertising creative directors were women (according to the organization's website, that number has since climbed to 11 percent). There were three women and one man on the panel. The audience was almost exclusively women.

Our conversation was wide-ranging and sometimes contentious: we talked about the implications of men sculpting women's insecurities to maximize corporate profits and how even a gender-blind application process isn't a perfect fix in a society that punishes feminine boldness and confidence.

Whenever talk turned toward solutions, the panel came back to mentorship: women lifting up other women. Assertiveness and leaning in and ironclad portfolios and marching into that interview and taking the space you deserve and changing the ratio and not letting Steve from accounting talk over you in the meeting.

During the closing question-and-answer period, a young woman stood up. "I'm sorry," she said, her voice electric with anger, "but all I've heard tonight are a bunch of things women can do to fight sexism. Why is that our job? We didn't build this system. This audience should be full of men."

I thought about that question when I sat on an all-female panel in front of a mostly female audience talking about how to fix gender bias in comedy. I think about it every time a reporter asks me how victims of internet trolling can make ourselves safer online. I think about it when abortion rights are framed as men's to take away but only women's to fight for. Naturally, I thought about it constantly as #MeToo ripped through entertainment and politics and our own families, illuminating the ubiquity and scale of male sexual entitlement.

#MeToo felt like an appropriately cinematic turn: It's the third act, and our heroine is angry. She's finally stepping into her power. The witches are coming. It was beautiful to watch.

But I keep returning to that old question. Men: What exactly is it that you do here?

One pervasive feature of the post-#MeToo landscape has been distraught men apologizing for their gender, fretting about old drunken hookups, and begging for guidance on what they can do to help. (Of course, it took only moments to transform a mass catharsis into an emotional labor factory.) Hey, you know what you could do to help? Everything.

How about Matt Damon refuses to show up to work until his female costars are paid as much as he is? How about Jimmy Fallon refuses to interview anyone who has been credibly accused of sexual assault or domestic violence? How about Robert Downey, Jr., relentlessly points out microaggressions against female contemporaries until he develops a reputation for being "difficult" and every day on Twitter four thousand eighth graders call him an "SJW cuck"? How about Harvey Weinstein anonymously donates $100 million to the Time's Up legal defense fund and then melts into the fog as though he never existed?

How about men boycott Twitter? How about men strike for International Women's Day? How about men take on the economic and social burdens of calling out toxic patterns of gendered socialization? How about anyone but the oppressed lifts a finger to change anything at all?

Sexism is a male invention. White supremacy is a white invention. Transphobia is a cisgender invention. So far, men have treated #MeToo like a bumbling dad in a detergent commercial: well intentioned but floundering, as though they are not the experts.

You are the experts.

Only 2.6 percent of construction workers are female. We did not install that glass ceiling, and it is not our responsibility to demolish it.

In the summer of 2017, some old friends invited me to appear on their podcast. They are two stand-up comedians in their midthirties—I know, the podcast comes as a shock—and their show was a kind of micro-focus group, investigating how to be better straight white dudes by picking the brains of guests who don't fit that description.

They wanted to know what people like me, for instance (fat, female, feminist) need from people like them (plausible extras in a Buffalo Wild Wings commercial). It was a sweet and, I think, encouraging idea.

"How to build a better white guy" is a conversation that could turn academic fast, replete with all the jargon that the sneering class finds so tedious: intersectionality, emotional labor, systemic oppression, the dreaded "privilege." But when I sat down with my friends, only one question sprang to mind, and it was personal, not pedantic:

"Do you ever stick up for me?"

That question had been quietly nagging at my friendships with men since "Grab 'em by the pussy." The sound of Billy Bush snickering as Donald Trump talked about women in the most dehumanizing terms had been devastating in its ease and in how little it had surprised me.

I know that my male friends are privy to those kinds of conversations, even if they don't take part in them. I also know that some of them do take part. I've heard, secondhand, about men I consider close friends complaining that their girlfriends are getting fat. I know that there are men I love who rank women by number. I know that they consider themselves to be good people who fundamentally care about women's safety and equality.

So if you care, how often do you say something? Maybe you'll confront your close friends, but what about more powerful men, famous men, cool men, men who could further your career?

"Do you ever stick up for me?" sounds childish, but I don't know that gussying up the sentiment in more sophisticated language would enhance its meaning. It isn't fun to be the one who speaks up.

Our society has engineered robust consequences for squeaky wheels, a verdant pantheon from eye rolls all the way up to physical violence. One of the subtlest and most pervasive is social ostracism: coding empathy as the fun killer, consideration for others as an embarrassing weakness, and dissenting voices as out-of-touch, bleeding-heart dweebs (at best). Coolness is a fierce disciplinarian.

A result is that, for the most part, the only people weathering those consequences are the ones who don't have the luxury of staying quiet. Women, already impeded and imperiled by sexism, also have to carry the social stigma of being feminist buzzkills if they call attention to it. People of color not only have to deal with racism; they also have to deal with white people labeling them "angry" or "hostile" or "difficult" for objecting.

What we could really use is some loud, unequivocal backup. Or, I guess, front-up. And not just in public, when the tide of opinion has already turned and a little "woke"-ness might benefit you—but in private, when it can hurt.

One of my podcasting friends told me that he does stick up for women in challenging situations, like testosterone-soaked comedy greenrooms, for instance, but complained, "I get mocked for it!"

Yes, I know you do. Welcome. Getting yelled at and made fun of is where many of us live all the time. Speaking up costs us friends, jobs, credibility, and invisible opportunities we'll never even know enough about to regret.

I know there's pressure not to be a dorky, try-hard male feminist stereotype; there's always a looming implication that you could lose your spot in the boys' club; if you seem opportunistic or performative in your support, if you suck up too much oxygen and demand praise, women will yell at you for that, too. But I need you to absorb that risk. I need you to get yelled at and made fun of, a lot, and if you get kicked out of the club, I need you to be relieved, and I need you to help build a new one.

Boundaries *work*. The angry white men of Gear Swap eventually did get fed up with all the "discrimination," the club's refusal to change for them, and kicked themselves out of the club. They took the moderators' advice to start their own gear swap—no communism allowed!—flouncing gloriously to their new land, where, much like those libertarians who bought some property in Chile and tried to make their own Galt's Gulch until they imploded because it turned out we actually have regulations and a coherent tax structure and checks on power for a reason, the Nu-Gear Swappers failed miserably.

To kick things off, the founder of Seattle Music Gear Swap and Sell (No Idpol, No Communists, No Fascists) posted this inspiring welcome message:

> After witnessing how race obsession and identity politics ruins everything it touches, I've decided to provide an alternative. Post your gear and requests. Race baiters will be banned.

As I write this, the group has seventeen members, all of whom are now banned from Seattle Music Gear Swap and Sale. There is one three-week-old post, advertising a bass, which has garnered no comments. There are three other posts, all of which are about how great it is to swap gear freely without identity politics getting in the way. Two of those have devolved into petty arguing.

No gear has been swapped at the time of this writing.

Seattle Music Gear Swap and Sale has 16,359 members. There are so many posts about gear that I could find no trace of the dust-up that birthed Seattle Music Gear Swap and Sell (No Idpol, No Communists, No Fascists) just a few weeks ago. Those men are lost to time to a new world, the world they thought they wanted.

Joan

Two ways in which I am a gender traitor:

One, and I know this is going to be tough for a lot of you to hear, but I don't give a shit about pockets. A coat should have pockets, for cold hands, but pockets on a dress are as useful to me as an electric can opener. Except that an electric can opener will increase in usefulness as I grow older and my joints deteriorate and I yearn more and more for soft peas. A pocket on a dress is a droopy, drape-ruining cotton-poly scrotum at any age.

I mean, pockets on a dress are great if you need to carry *one fingernail clipping.* Pockets on a dress are great if you're living that two-dimensional tesseract life and need to transport a line. Finally! I don't have to carry a purse when I go to the faerie market to trade this daisy for a hummingbird's kiss! At last, portable storage for my single red acetate fortune-telling fish. But put a wallet and keys and concert tickets and a lipstick in there—i.e., the things that would make a pocket useful—and, congrats, you've grown two great clonking thigh cysts, a feast for thieves.

I can't count the number of times I've been drawn into the old dance, both parts: someone compliments my dress, and I announce, "It has pockets!" as though "pockets" were German for "a time machine to go give Mitch McConnell's dad a condom"; or I compliment someone else's dress, am informed of pockets, and squeal like Mitch McConnell's dad dooming the future of humanity with one squirt. I participate; I am complicit. But this is a post-#MeToo society, this is International Year of the Woman (is it? I don't know), this is my time, down here, and I do not care to do it anymore.

"Nice dress!"

"Thank you—it has pockets!!!!!!"

"Yes, I can see that, as you look like you have chunky Mr. Tumnus hocks under there."

Pockets in a dress are so Zooey Deschanel can always have a crystal nearby. Pockets in a dress are just in case Maggie Gyllenhaal finds a four-leaf clover. Pockets in a dress are for baby girl who is best fwiends with a bee and need one sugared violet for dinner in case she get wost chasing dandelion fuzz. That should be a niche market *at best*, not a foundational trope of womanhood.

The feminine directive to love pockets is a cheap simulacrum of gender solidarity where none really exists. They are used to distract us from harnessing our real power and I, for one, am no longer willing to be in the pocket of Big Pocket! Brag to me about your pockets when they're FILLED WITH UNION PAMPHLETS AND FREE TAMPONS FOR THE HOMELESS.

Anyhoo, the second way in which I am a Bad Woman is that I know I am supposed to be very engorged for her, but Joan Rivers never made me feel anything but shitty.

I was a full baby when Joan was at her peak as a regular guest host on Johnny Carson's *Tonight Show* in the early 1980s, and a very recent baby when she left in 1986 to helm *The Late Show Starring Joan Rivers*, an ill-fated nighttime talk show on Fox. After Joan finally, briefly got her own hosting gig, Carson famously never spoke to her again—outraged that she would dare to reach for more, more than just being his pet, more than waiting for a chance in *the chair*, a chance that would probably never come because only men are real.

Joan came into my consciousness a bit later—the nineties and aughts—specifically her awards show coverage for E! with her daughter, Melissa, and later, her frequently brutal panel show *Fashion Police*. (I was, for reasons lost to me now, a passionate E!-head as a child.*)

---

* At the 2018 Oscars I discovered I was leaning on a cocktail table next to nineties E! correspondent Jerry Penacoli and freaked the fuck out on him, only to realize midfreak that I didn't actually have much of an opinion about nineties E! correspondent Jerry Penacoli. Sorry you had to take that journey with me, Jerry.

Joan seemed, to adolescent me, a sort of barking bailiff of the patriarchy—enforcing cruel judgments about which women were allowed to show their arms, whose ass was too fat, who should stop kidding herself, who was trying too hard, who would be alone forever. Of course, at the time, I barely knew the term *patriarchy* and certainly didn't make distinctions between patriarchal norms and objective truth; I had no self outside the system. Joan, in that context, was bad for me. She found something wrong with not just every woman but every movie star. If Kate Winslet wasn't beautiful, what was I? And Joan was a woman herself. She wasn't Howard Stern. She was speaking from a place not of horniness but of realism. Howard often made me feel like shit; Joan consistently made me certain I was.

On *The Howard Stern Show* in 2008, Joan said, of the way Lena Dunham used her body on *Girls*: "Don't make yourself, physically—don't let them laugh at you physically. Don't say it's okay that other girls can look like this. Try to look better!"

My friend Guy Branum worked for Joan Rivers on *Fashion Police*, writing jokes around a dining room table at her daughter, Melissa's, house. At the time, the HBO show *Girls* was everywhere, so its star and creator, Dunham, was, too.

"I got to be in the room while Joan was processing Lena Dunham," Guy told me. "Lena Dunham was this object of fascination for her, because here you had someone who in Joan's eyes was certainly dumpier than she was, and she was successful but she wasn't scared."

Working for Joan at that time, as part of a staff of women and gay men, was both an incredible opportunity for marginalized writers and one for which they were so underpaid they eventually went on strike. Joan was not a hero or a mentor. She was of the system that had been cruel to her, and questions of if and how Joan lifted up younger comics are complicated. What wasn't complicated is how Joan viewed Lena Dunham: she was breaking all the miserable rules made by men that Joan felt she had no choice but to follow.

Guy explained, "Not only was Lena surviving, but she was putting herself physically and sexually out there in a way that Joan didn't think was possible."

Whether through a failure of imagination or will, or out of sheer pragmatism, Joan couldn't see a Joan outside the system any better than I could imagine a liberated self at age fourteen. For nearly sixty years she propped up that structure as passionately as she denounced it, a willing caryatid who hated every ounce bearing down on her, spitting defiantly up at the lintel and counting the drips as profits.

"She didn't understand having the power to decide how much you're going to let the world tell you who you are," Guy said.

Can you imagine if she had? If we're calling voiciness a kind of witchcraft, then Joan was the Grand High Witch. She just never quite landed in the truth.

There's a scene in the documentary *Joan Rivers: A Piece of Work*, which came out in 2010, when Joan was seventy-seven years old, where she reluctantly agrees to be the subject of a Comedy Central Roast. But, she laments, and her terror is visceral, they're going to be so cruel, they're going to talk about her age, her body, her plastic surgery, her washed-up career. It's a good thing the money is "extraordinary." It's a jarring moment of vulnerability from a woman who abstractly hosted the roast of Lindy West's giant butt every night of my adolescence (and I didn't even get "extraordinary" money for it!). How could Joan have the gall to publicly yearn for the kind of humanity she refused to extend to others? Or, a far better question, why did she ultimately decide she wasn't worthy of that humanity and subject herself to the roast anyway?

I call Joan a bailiff because one of her more baffling ideological consistencies was that she never presented herself as the judge, merely as the enforcer. She was just telling you what she's learned from experience. Get real. Wise up.

"Joan felt so hurt by the world," Guy told me. "She felt so certain that she didn't have what it takes to be respected, and she was going to point out everyone else's inadequacies because she was sure that hers were very evident."

Guy came to Joan a little bit earlier than I did. His

Joan period began, he said, around the time that she was making fat jokes about Shelley Winters and Elizabeth Taylor—Hollywood royalty who had dared get older and, yes, bigger. "As an eight-year-old I thought, oh, those women are fat," Guy said. "What I didn't understand was that when Joan was a twenty-year-old, those women were beauty."

That was the thing about Joan, the hardest thing. It was that *she knew*. She knew how it felt. She was a woman born in 1933 who aspired to fame in a field so dominated by men that "women aren't funny" was still conventional wisdom the day she died in 2014. She was a woman in show business, an industry so fixated on one narrow version of female perfection that she herself underwent 348 cosmetic procedures.

She was a woman in the world.

She knew what it took from you. On *The Ed Sullivan Show* in 1967, Joan (beautiful, slim, confident in a beehive and a black dress) eviscerated sexist double standards with a clarity and indignation that, from both a political and a comedic standpoint, would absolutely hold up today:

> The whole society is not for single girls, you know that. Single men, yes. A man, he's single, he's so lucky. A boy on a date, all he has to be is clean and able to pick up the check, he's a winner, you know that. . . . A girl has to be well dressed, face has to

> look nice, the hair has to be in shape. The girl has to be the one that's bright and pretty, intelligent, a good sport. . . . A girl, you're thirty years old, you're not married, you're an old maid. A man, he's ninety years old, he's not married, he's a catch. . . . A man in this society, as long as he's alive he's a catch.

Joan was that old maid, that was her joke. She was, as she famously said, the "last girl in Larchmont." She called herself ugly, fat, unfuckable—brutally honest about her worth in the eyes of a rigged society, but then, instead of fighting for us lost, last girls, she turned around and gave worse than she got. Men built the system, they run it, and we suffer (Joan was always clear on that), but if suffering's our lot, the best we can do is climb to the top of the pile, figure out how to get paid, how to be the one. And so Joan climbed us and climbed us and climbed us until she died, still not at the top.

"To her, the shit you talked at beautiful people was part of you acknowledging that you would never be beautiful in that way," Guy said, "while at the same time you were supposed to always be trying very hard to be beautiful in that way, if that makes any sense to you."

Yes, it makes perfect sense to me. Talking shit at the system is halfway to being free, which I suppose is better than nothing.

In decades past, if you were a woman trying to make it in the male-dominated, male-controlled, male-gate-kept world of comedy, there were essentially two options: break or bend.

You could refuse to contort yourself, to make yourself smaller, to endorse the lie of scarcity—that there can be only one woman in the club, one chill Smurfette.* You could call that bluff and tell the truth about how they talk to you, look at you, touch you, book you, promote you (or don't). You could revolt and say, "No. Here is what I deserve. Here is what I demand. Here is what I will not tolerate." You could tell your male colleagues that perhaps you shouldn't have to sit through a litany of rape jokes and "take my wife" boilerplate night after night after night just to do your job. You could suggest that perhaps a monoculture entirely saturated with and policed by men might not be a reliable arbiter of whether or not women are funny. You could decline to look at Louis CK's penis and maybe even complain about it to someone important. You could mentor younger women and bring them up behind you to undercut the lie that there is only one spot.

---

* Also, that Smurfette comparison is very good, because Gargamel is one of those classic effete, confirmed bachelor, gay-coded, fun-ruining villains (aka male feminist soy boy cuck), and Azrael is a literal pussy (aka bitch woman), and all they do is scheme and connive to catch and boil (aka DO CALL-OUT CULTURE ON) all the cool Smurf boys who are just trying to ease tension and lighten the mood in Smurf Village, man! Give me an award for this metaphor.

And then, in return for your efforts, you could be labeled a moral scold, an unfunny feminazi bitch, the PC police, the wrong fit, a bad comic, and a bad sport, and you could fade slowly out of your chosen career, your home, your friend group, and your coping mechanism and diminish and go back to school for physical therapy and open a nice little practice somewhere and be the funniest one in book club. Oh, I used to do comedy, but I don't anymore.

Or you could be Joan. You could kill those parts of yourself that hope for more. You could laugh along with your own dehumanization and agree that's it's okay because it's "just a joke," the sacred joke. You could say the worst things quicker and louder to prove that you're not like other girls, you won't kill the vibe. You could claim your spot in the boys' club, nearest the door, first one gone if you step out of line, and you could defend that square of tile venomously—not against men but against other women—for the rest of your life. You could learn, ultimately, that the boys will never truly let you into the club, and even if they worship you it's as a novelty and it's temporary and conditional as hell.

And you could work a thousand times harder than your male colleagues for a thousandth of the respect, until your incredible work ethic becomes part of your mythos. *A Piece of Work* lingers, enraptured, over Joan's legendary card catalogs full of jokes, floor to ceiling in her penthouse, sixty years of jokes, every joke she's ever written, meticulously categorized—as though that kind of drive is all pluck and no terror. Joan would famously take any job ("I'll write for Hitler for five hundred dollars," she told Terry Gross in 2012), a prolificity that was of course used against her, to cheapen her reputation.

It must also be said: some combination of the sheer amount of material she committed herself to producing, the boys' club maxim "funny is funny," and an innate brutality in her own comic sensibilities, led Joan to some truly horrific material, well beyond calling Liz Taylor a hippo. In 2014, when asked if she thought we'd see a gay president before a female president, Joan said, "We already have it with Obama, so let's just calm down. You know Michelle is a tr*nny." She then clarified: "A transgender. We all know it." On the Golden Globes red carpet in 2006, she announced, "This is the sixty-third Golden Globe Awards, or, for our friends in China, the Groden Grobies! Herro!"

It is so cruel to make great things and take them away in the same breath.

In person she could be kind and vulnerable; her favorite flowers were yellow roses; she loved her fans and her family; she was devoted to the gay community; she always wanted to be an actress, not a comic. She was a magical person who was put into an impossible situation, who frequently said inexcusable things, who showed young women—myself included—a version of womanhood we didn't know was possible, just how powerful and funny and excellent and strong a woman could be, and she used our fascination, our rapturous attention, to brutalize us. In her way, she mentored every loud, disobedient misfit just by being there, working, killing, bombing, getting up again, living, excelling until her last day.

Joan fell into so many traps that society sets for women, and her failures and frailties mapped those pits so that those who came after could avoid them. But it should always be our goal not to perpetuate what is inflicted upon us. Your pain may not be fair, but it's yours.

Guy told me a story from the *Fashion Police* writers room, when drag queen and writer Jackie Beat asked Joan what she thought of Totie Fields, another pioneering female comic of the 1960s and '70s. "What Jackie was looking for was some sort of lovely collegiality or mentorship or some sort of connection between them," he explained. Instead, Joan recalled, as soon as Fields identified her as competition, she did her best to make sure Joan would never, ever work in Vegas. Joan eventually did play Vegas, but "it was a long, hard struggle because of the shit that Totie Fields pulled."

"It was an interesting moment of realizing that Joan completely came from a world where there can be only one, and that was being defined by people around her as much as it was being defined by her," Guy said. "And you could feel the hurt and the fight in her voice as it was coming out." That wasn't the story that Jackie or Guy, both of whom worshipped both Joan and Totie, wanted to hear, but it was the truth. It's not the truth anymore, partly because of Joan and partly despite her.

Despite Joan's vocal loathing of being called a pioneer ("I'm not ready to be an icon, and I'm not ready to be told thank you!" she hollered in *A Piece of Work*), she objectively did carve a path, an easier one than hers, for the women behind her. She had to give up every single thing to make room for herself, and that messy, blazing, cruel sacrifice made it possible for other women to take her place without the same self-negation.

"She fucking locked some doors behind her, I will never question that," Guy told me.

He was quiet for a moment.

"I think," he said, "that if Joan stands for anything, isn't it your right to talk shit about people who made you feel like garbage? Which is why I've always found her empowering."

You can hate someone and love them at the same time. Maybe that's a natural side effect of searching for heroes in a world not built for you.

Obsolescence Is a Preventable Disease

One time, in the '90s, Adam Carolla said, "I pick my nose like it powers my car."

I think about "I pick my nose like it powers my car" every time I pick my nose and every time I drive my car, so multiple times per day. It's so funny—such a perfectly revelatory little detail, indulgently defiant of Middle American manners, celebrating one of the base pleasures of having a body and inviting the audience to throw off propriety and confess, too. My love for Adam Carolla started in my early teens, with *Loveline*, and carried through the first half of my twenties as he transitioned into a morning show (a welcome development for me when Howard Stern moved to satellite radio) and, eventually, a podcast.

In the early days, Carolla was still a relative unknown, whose previous life as a blue-collar worker hadn't yet been supplanted by his new identity as a Literal Millionaire and who'd found his way to *Loveline* after offering his services as a boxing coach to a pre–*Win Ben Stein's Money* Jimmy Kimmel. He was just a guy. And it's easy to dispute this in hindsight, but I'm telling you, Carolla was very good at the radio. He was a virtuosic observer, weaving riffs on society's hypocrisies, and his own, with genuine compassion for *Loveline*'s callers. But there was always a discomforting edge: vicious jokes about the feckless poor (but it's okay because he grew up poor!), gleeful stereotyping of Latinos (but they're his buddies from the construction site!) and women and fat people and gay people and trans people (but he makes fun of everyone equally!), which only became less playful and pliable as Carolla grew older and richer.

I got older, too, my conscience matured and solidified, and eventually I realized that the taste of it had changed in my mouth. "Common sense" without growth, curiosity, or perspective eventually becomes conservatism and bitterness. I moved on.

There are pieces of pop culture that you outgrow because you get older. Then there are pieces of pop culture that you outgrow because you get better. Or rather the world gets better. The world moves forward. Not in secret, not in ambush, but in front of our faces. Everyone has the choice to listen and absorb, or to shut down and dig in.

As a child I loved Roseanne Barr so much, and just the knowledge of her existence out there—as a fat, funny, defiant, loud woman—bolstered my fat, funny, shrinking, quiet adolescence. It never occurred to me that twenty years later Roseanne would call me a "fat bitch" on Twitter for critiquing misogyny in comedy, which she perceived as "advocating censorship."

The Simpsons are the original high bar of comedy: surreal, subversive, yet emotionally alive. White kids my age never had to wonder about the impact of Apu on our South Asian classmates, and "white privilege" wasn't in the mainstream lexicon yet (let alone pervasive enough to warrant a reactionary sneering backlash from Adam Carolla).

Many people—myself included, at one time—consider Louis CK to be one of the greatest living stand-up comics, an astute, self-effacing, disgusting, loving dad who managed to win over not just the morning talk radio boys' club but tougher crowds such as feminists and art snobs (probably because none of us paid attention to what he was saying to the talk radio boys' club). His 2013 HBO special *Oh My God* was praised for its frank acknowledgment of rape culture (acknowledgment may be a low bar, but it was all we had in the pre-Cosby landscape). In what, at the time, was catnip for feminist bloggers, Louis CK called men "the number one cause of injury and mayhem to women" and pointed out that for women, spending time alone with a man requires "courage."

I suppose he would know.

I was in college in Los Angeles—still shy, ungainly, unsettled—when the British *Office* came out. I remember watching it for the first time, hunched over my ancient laptop in my mouse-infested room in my black widow–infested house, and thinking "I never knew." I'd been a comedy obsessive all my life, but I was young. It had never clicked before. I'd never known that comedy could be so perfect and efficient. I'd never put it together that if you make a piece of writing very, very funny you can take it very, very dark. The power of humor to manipulate an audience's thinking, to make surgically precise points, and the responsibility that goes along with that—the responsibility to always watch where you're punching—I learned that from Ricky Gervais. Not so many years later, Gervais would suggest that supermarkets make their doors smaller so that fat people cannot access the food.

Art has no obligation to evolve, but it has a powerful incentive to do so. Art that is static, that captures a dead moment, is nothing. It is, at best, nostalgia; at worst, it can be a blight on our sense of who we are, a shame we pack away. Artists who refuse to listen, participate, and change along with the world around them are not being silenced or punished by censorious college sophomores. They are letting obsolescence devour them, voluntarily. Political correctness is just the inexorable turn of the gear. Falling behind is preventable.

But so many people are fighting that turn of the gear. Gervais, for example, insists that he does not care what you say about him on Twitter. He does not care if you are offended. He does not care if you hate the latest joke he told about rape or the Bible or Caitlyn Jenner or Hitler or your child's fatal peanut allergy. And just to make sure you're crystal clear on all of the tweets he does not remotely care about, he built his 2018 Netflix stand-up special, *Ricky Gervais: Humanity*, around them—those negligible tweets, the droning of gnats, several years of which he appears to have accidentally screen grabbed and saved to his phone. (Ricky Gervais: butterfingers!)

Similarly, I don't care about Formula One racing, which is why I'm working on a tight seventy-five about the Abu Dhabi Grand Prix.

Gervais seems to care quite intensely, of course, which is natural. It would be grotesque, inhuman, not to care. Absorbing critique on a scale as vast as Gervais's Twitter feed (13.1 million followers), whether the specific critiques are warranted or not, is objectively grueling. Doing stand-up comedy is vulnerable and hard. Twitter is Hell. Devoid of context, Gervais's bravado might be sympathetic, a relatable if tedious coping mechanism. As Gervais himself helpfully pointed out in *Humanity*, however, nothing can truly be divorced from context.

"People see something they don't like, and they expect it to stop," he said. "The world is getting worse. Don't get me wrong, I think I've lived through the best fifty years of humanity, 1960 through 2015, the peak of civilization for everything. For tolerances, for freedoms, for communication, for medicine! And now it's going the other way a little bit."

"Dumpster fire" has emerged as the favorite emblem of our present sociopolitical moment, but that Gervais quote feels both more apt and more tragic as metaphor: the Trump/Brexit era is a rich, famous, white, middle-aged man declaring the world to be in decline the moment he stops understanding it.

I had the chance to interview Carolla for *The Stranger* in 2010, years after I'd soured on his work but before he'd turned quite as hard-line antisnowflake as he is now. I still held some vestige of youthful nostalgia for the good part of Adam, the part that at least always wanted to hear everyone's story, and I was curious to see if I could talk to that guy.

It took little prompting from me before he was off on a rant:

> As far as the feminist stuff goes, or the gay movement, or the black movement, or the Hispanic movement, or something—you see, people mistake being against the general movement for being against the people. Like, I want women to have equal rights and access to abortions and lesbians should be able to get married and women should get equal pay for equal work and all that shit. I'm

> just so fucking tired of recognizing everyone's group. That's the whole point. All these groups, by the way, would be much better off without their groups. The people would be better off without their groups. Yeah, fucking Jesse Jackson and Al Sharpton are working wonders in the black community. Man, have they really turned things around. Imagine where they'd be without them. Fuckin' ridiculous. These guys are professional extortionists—that's all they are. The only group that should matter is your fuckin' family.

I asked, sincerely, how he proposed that oppressed people advocate for themselves, fight to make their lives better, without some form of collective action.

"Oh, without a group?" He paused for a long time. "Yeah, well, how do you get off the ground with a topic like gay marriage, or how do you push an agenda like gay marriage if you don't have a group to back that? That's a valid point."

"Because that seems like the most effective means to get people to shut up," I said.

"Yeah. I would love the gays to marry so they could shut up."

He was right there, so close to taking a step into the future. But our phone call ended, and so did that moment, that crystal of potential.

In July 2017, Carolla announced that he was producing a documentary called *No Safe Spaces* with conservative radio host Dennis Prager, which "exposes the dangerous trend of suppressing free speech" on America's college campuses. "Trigger warnings, micro-aggressions, the suppression of free speech, and other illogical ideas born on campuses are proliferating and spreading out into the real world," the film's IndieGoGo page reads. "Today's campus snowflake is tomorrow's teacher, judge, or elected official. And if that doesn't scare you, maybe you should reconsider. No matter where you live or what you do, if you don't think the way they do, they will attempt to silence and punish you."

Adam Carolla is a multimillionaire who holds the Guinness World Record for "most downloaded podcast" and has published two *New York Times* best-selling books. Clearly the snowflakes have done their worst.

Carolla isn't angry because he's being silenced; he's angry because he's being challenged. He's been shown the road map to continued relevance, and it doesn't lead straight back to his mansion. He's angry because he's being asked to do the basic work of maintaining a shared humanity or else be left behind. He's choosing the past.

Gervais and Carolla are not alone in presenting themselves as noble bulwarks against a wave of supposed left-wing censorship. (A Netflix special, for the record, is not what "silencing" looks like.) We've heard similar sentiments from handwringers across the political spectrum who insist that overzealous, "politically correct" college activists are strangling academia. We've heard it from pundits and politicians who insist that white men have been so victimized by the "sensitivity" of marginalized people that they had no choice but to vote for Donald Trump.

In November 2017, following a *New York Times* report detailing CK's proclivity for (among other things) masturbating in front of female colleagues, CK announced that he was retreating from the public eye to "take a long time to listen." Nine months later he performed an unannounced set at the Comedy Cellar in New York, reportedly to a standing ovation. Four months after that, an audience member surreptitiously recorded CK working on new material at a Long Island comedy club and leaked the audio online.

On the tape, CK delivered an extended riff on the supposed self-seriousness of the survivors of the Parkland school shooting: "Fuck you. That's not interesting. Because you went to a high school where kids got shot? Why does that mean I gotta listen to you? Why does that make you interesting? You didn't get shot. You pushed some fat kid in the way and now I gotta listen to you talk?"

Less than a year after his vow to retreat and listen, CK made the laziest and most cowardly choice possible: to turn away from the difficult, necessary work of self-reflection, growth, and reparation, and run into the comforting arms of people who don't think it's that big a deal to show your penis to female subordinates. Conservatives adore a disgraced liberal who's willing to pander to them because he's too weak to grow. How pathetic to take them up on it.

If you've spent any time with Gervais's work beyond *The Office* and *Extras*, you know that the man is obsessed with evolution. His 2003 stand-up special was about animals; his 2010 special was called *Science*; in 2009 and 2010, he released special episodes of his podcast, *The Ricky Gervais Show*, devoted to natural history, the human body, the earth.

On their Xfm radio show in the early 2000s, Gervais and his cohost, Stephen Merchant, did a recurring segment called "Do We Need 'Em?" in which the producer, Karl Pilkington, chose an animal he found strange or useless (jellyfish, for instance) and interviewed a scientist about whether or not we should "keep" them.

"What are they adding to the world?" he once asked Gervais and Merchant about giraffes. "What are they doing?"

Gervais explained that species aren't here because they add something to the world. They weren't chosen by a benevolent creator; they aren't the most beautiful or the strongest or the most beneficial to the whole. They just didn't die. They survived to pass on their genetic material, and that's it. That's evolution. The world thunders on, with or without you. Adapt or perish.

It's baffling that Gervais can have so much reverence for physical evolution and so little for intellectual evolution.

He might find trans people silly, but you know who doesn't? Teenagers. I remember the first gay kiss on TV, and I am only thirty-seven years old; my kids think I must be exaggerating. My husband, a stand-up comic, used to do a bit about a Comcast commercial in which a woman goes on a date with a little green alien and, it is implied, fucks him; at the time, interracial human couples were taboo in advertising. That joke doesn't work anymore, because the world changed and it's going to keep changing.

I'm being hard on Ricky Gervais not because his attitude is extraordinary but because it is common. Not because I think he and the other ostensibly left-leaning men who succumb to this trap are just like Trump but because I believe they aren't. Or they don't have to be.

You can choose to be permeable, to be curious, to be the one that didn't die.

What Is an Abortion, Anyway?

From the first moment I started to believe that Hollywood might actually let me turn my memoir, *Shrill*, into a TV show, I knew I wanted an abortion in there. I brought it up in every single meeting, with stranger after stranger, in the earliest meet-and-greets with production companies that weren't even sure they wanted the option yet—the seduction-stage meetings, when a master tactician might suggest that one *not* say the word "abortion" forty-seven times over calamari at Soho House West Hollywood. But I needed people to know what they would be getting if they optioned the book: we're putting an abortion in the pilot, and we're doing it right. If they didn't want to do that, they weren't making my show.

Annie Easton, the character loosely based on me in the TV version of *Shrill* (which we eventually sold to Hulu, a pantheon of kings and queens whose unequivocal support of our abortion episode I would gladly repay with my firstborn child, if I ever choose to have one), gets pregnant by her loser boy-man hookup because she is having fun, reckless, unprotected, recreational sex, and then she has an abortion because she does not want to be pregnant and wanting an abortion is the same as needing an abortion.

Annie goes to Planned Parenthood (we shot the sequence at a real Planned Parenthood in a suburb of Portland, Oregon), where she receives kind, competent, nonjudgmental care from a team of providers, who help her end her pregnancy smoothly and quickly with her best friend at her side. After her abortion, Annie feels relieved, grateful, and powerful. She is the author of her own life. She was not forced to bear a child.

That's what my real abortion was like, except that I went to the clinic alone, which might not have been the case had I seen an episode of television like the pilot of *Shrill.* Maybe I would have done things differently if I'd known you could bring a support person in with you, if I'd known my abortion didn't need to be a secret I experienced in total isolation, if I'd known what abortion really is: a profound act of care that affirms a pregnant person's innate, inviolable freedom.

Annie is not every person who has ever gotten an abortion. She is white and she has health insurance and she's broke but not poor and she lives in a state where no one made her wait forty-eight hours and submit to a pelvic ultrasound and stare at a sonogram image in order to obtain medical care to which she is fundamentally entitled both under the US Constitution and, regardless of law, as an autonomous human being with free will. Millions of people in the United States do not have Annie's good fortune, and their freedom and safety are imperiled more each day under the Trump regime. But Annie is like many, many people who have abortions and whose experiences are vastly underrepresented in media and public discourse; she is a lot like me.

At the clinic, an actor playing a doctor tells Annie (and everyone watching at home), "You might feel some light cramping, you might also feel some numbing."

Aidy Bryant, as Annie, stares at the ceiling, biting her lip.

"Some cramping is normal," the doctor says.

Everything about the scene is normal. You just might not know that from television.

The short history of abortion on our TV and movie screens goes something like this: it didn't exist as an option at all, it became a shameful secret; it became a dangerous punishment for a fallen woman; it became one side of a debate; it became an option discussed very briefly and then dismissed—or not mentioned at all, even when a teenager was unexpectedly pregnant. Many plotlines that seemed to be heading toward abortion ended instead in eleventh-hour miscarriages, sparing the protagonist the supposedly agonizing and morally compromising choice, allowing her to remain "likable" in a wholly uncomplicated way.

The first abortion I ever remember seeing on screen was that of Penny in *Dirty Dancing*, who is nearly killed by an unscrupulous opportunist with a "rusty knife" who promises he can end her pre–*Roe v. Wade* pregnancy. Penny is not quite blamed for getting herself into "trouble"—in fact, she receives tender, lifesaving care from Jerry Orbach, oddly one of the most affecting depictions of an abortion care provider ever committed to film—but her story is gruesome and traumatic nonetheless. The next fictional abortion that had an impact on me I never actually saw at all. On the Canadian teen soap *Degrassi: The Next Generation* (which I watched religiously with my college roommates because IT WAS GOOD), a teenage girl named Manny decides to have an abortion in a two-part episode called "Accidents Will Happen." The US network that aired *Degrassi* refused to run that episode—not, as I understand it, because Manny had an abortion but because she had an abortion and didn't regret it. That was in 2004.

Shrill wasn't the first show to put an abortion on TV, but I believe it was the first to feature an abortion in a pilot episode, and it joined a short list of shows that have presented abortion without high drama, anguish, or regret, as well as shows that have opted to take viewers through the procedure itself. I'm very proud of our choice. At the close of my career, whenever that comes, Annie's abortion just may be the thing I'm most proud of.

Funny, because I never planned to write about my abortion at all.

In the fall of 2015, I was in the thick of writing *Shrill* the book—my deadline was looming, and I was embarrassingly behind and starting to imagine doomsday scenarios in which I would have to pay back my advance and go into hiding. At the same time, national hysteria about Planned Parenthood selling "baby parts" was at its peak, and my feminist friends and I were vacillating between rage and panic over it.

I was in self-imposed writing exile at a friend's vacation home in Maine when my friend Amelia Bonow texted me, "I just told everyone on Facebook about my abortion! SORRY, FAMILY! LOLZ."

Earlier that summer, Amelia and I had told each other about our abortions for the first time, which had gotten me thinking about why so few of my friends knew about mine. I wasn't traumatized by my abortion, which I'd had in 2010, or ashamed of it. It had made my life better. Amelia felt the same way. It was just something you weren't supposed to talk about. We noticed that people almost never said the word at all. And if we were bowing to that imposed secrecy in liberal, pro-choice Seattle, did that mean that all sorts of people are just having abortions all the time and pretending that they're not? If that is the default way to have an abortion in one of the most progressive parts of the country, how much is internalized stigma still determining the way pro-choice people relate to their own abortions?

Amelia and I realized that the only people who felt free to talk about abortions in specifics were those advocating for its eradication—and their specifics were lies and propaganda. Why weren't we owning our own stories? Why were we caving to a stigma that we didn't even believe in?

Stigma breeds silence, and silence is a vacuum that abortion opponents can fill with whatever stories they want. I realized in that conversation with Amelia that despite growing up in progressive Seattle, with a mom who was a nurse *who performed abortions*, sometimes having to step in when other nurses refused, I had heard very little truth about abortion. The most progressive line when I was growing up was "safe, legal, and rare." Abortion was a "complicated debate." Pro-choicers assiduously insisted that "nobody is pro-abortion." People who got abortions were either desperate or irresponsible. I didn't hear any stories like mine—abortions that weren't traumatic, that weren't regretted or obtained under desperate circumstances, but were just young pregnant people exercising their rights to steer their own futures.

A few months after that conversation, when I was off in Maine, Amelia and I and a few friends had been batting around the idea of an abortion storytelling night or a

YouTube channel for abortion stories, when, in a spasm of frustration, she went ahead and posted her story on social media. It read:

> Hi guys! Like a year ago I had an abortion at the Planned Parenthood on Madison Ave, and I remember this experience with a nearly inexpressible level of gratitude. . . . Plenty of people still believe that on some level—if you are a good woman—abortion is a choice which should [be] accompanied by some level of sadness, shame, or regret. But you know what? I have a good heart and having an abortion made me happy in a totally unqualified way. Why wouldn't I be happy that I was not forced to become a mother?

I tell this story onstage with some regularity. I choke up every time I get to "I have a good heart and having an abortion made me happy." It happened just now as I typed this, even after all these years. Amelia does have a good heart. How inhumane, to teach people that they are bad for being free.

"This is amazing," I texted back, and I asked if I could post a screen grab to my then eighty thousand or so Twitter followers. Something in this observation, that even the unashamed speak of abortion only in whispers, clicked with me and I added the hashtag #ShoutYourAbortion.

It immediately took off. People from all over the world began sharing their own stories. Amelia and I began hearing from women who'd been suicidal over the shame of their abortions and felt free for the first time—and not only free but part of a global community declaring sovereignty over their bodies. We heard from women in religious countries who'd had illegal abortions and risked ostracism by their families, or even violence or incarceration, if they spoke openly about owning their bodies and futures. We heard from women who'd had to abort nonviable fetuses at twenty-four weeks who were tired of their personal trauma being used as a bargaining chip by Republicans. We heard from trans men who had been victims of sexual assault and in seeking their abortions had been forced to weather the compounded traumas of rape, gender dysphoria, and erasure. We heard from defiant high school students and wise elders and our own mothers. The hashtag dominated twitter for days and was covered by what felt like every major media source, landing on page one of the *New York Times* a couple weeks after the original post. Clearly, this was more than a hashtag. Clearly there was a need here—a yearning to talk.

Not everyone felt liberated by or pleased with the conversation. Amelia and I received lots of messages that opened with the phrase, "I'm pro-choice, but . . ." One reality that SYA had kicked to the surface was that the pro-choice movement was really, REALLY not on the same page about how people are supposed to talk about their abortions. The anti-choice people, on the other hand, were predictably monolithic in their, um, criticisms of SYA. In spite of the fact that only 23 percent of Americans want to see *Roe v. Wade* reversed and the anti-choice movement comprises a sliver of the US population, the word cloud of "abortion discourse in the last two decades" has been about 90 percent white evangelicals screaming the most incendiary, reductive, poisonous garbage imaginable in lockstep with one another. The brand is strong!

It is easy to craft an impenetrable brand when you are lying. Anti-choice rhetoric generally falls into three categories:

1. Extremely oversimplified and totally subjective ("Life begins at conception").
2. So incendiary that all who disagree are immediately marked as evil ("Abortion is murder").
3. An oxygen-less loop of tautology ("Life begins at conception, therefore abortion is murder").

The pro-choice movement, on the other hand, has never figured out an effective way to counteract anti-abortion propaganda because the omnipresence of that propaganda has terrified the vast majority of people who have abortions into silence and because for decades we have constantly been allowing ourselves to be drawn into a bad-faith debate over a fundamental human freedom that is not debatable. As soon as we are baited into correcting our opponents, it legitimizes their argument. Once you are arguing from the defense, you've already lost.

When Republicans introduce anti-abortion measures with no exceptions for rape or incest, the Left gestures, apoplectic, at the most barbaric hypotheticals—"You would force an eleven-year-old to carry her rapist's child?"—as though there is some threshold of age or circumstance or tragedy beyond which it is acceptable to force a person to have a baby. We rail against Republican legislation proposing a total abortion ban, and then, when lawmakers pass a twenty-week ban instead, they look moderate (by design).

We fall into the trap of qualifying certain abortion restrictions as more extreme or more inhumane than others, when the unshakable reality is that if you are a person who is unable to access abortion for any reason, your state is total disenfranchisement and your right to life has been stripped from you. Even when we insist, however valiantly, that "abortion is health care," we are playing into the devastating anti-choice fiction that abortion is anything less than liberty itself.

There is no debate because we do not live in a theocracy and one minority group does not get to implement legislation that impedes other people's freedom, period.

It is time to stop granting those people even one iota of our collective energy and instead begin flooding the world with our real, true, messy, complex, hard, good, bad abortion stories, because those stories are the things that actually happened to us and they are the things that people actually relate to, and that other shit is blatant horseshit to anyone who isn't an evangelical Christian cultist.

In the first debate of the 2016 presidential election, Donald Trump turned abortion into an *American Idol* origin story: "[W]hat happened is friends of mine years ago were going to have a child, and it was going to be aborted. And it wasn't aborted. And that child today is a total superstar, a great, great child. And I saw that. And I saw other instances."

Nonaborted *total* superstar. Even something as fundamental as women's humanity has to be turned into a game show. We would let you have autonomy over your own bodies, but that fetus you're incubating might be the next Bo Bice!

Friends. That is not a serious person. We must stop treating it like one.

On January 20, 2017, Trump's inauguration day, I had the surreal experience of giving the keynote speech at a fund-raiser for the Emma Goldman Clinic, an independent abortion care provider in Iowa City, Iowa. I had never been to Iowa before, and I arrived at the theater that night in a state of deep misunderstanding. I knew that Iowa had gone red for Trump. I believed, naively, that I had flown there to comfort *them*.

What I found was exactly the opposite: a group of people not drowning in shock and despair, as I was, but putting one foot in front of the other with grace and good humor, just as they had the day before and would the day after. Welcome, they said. We have already been living in Trump's America. We call it America.

The staff of the Emma Goldman Clinic knew well that the crisis surrounding abortion access in this country predates Donald Trump. Although most people think of Planned Parenthood when they think of abortion, independent providers like the Emma Goldman Clinic perform 60 percent of abortion procedures nationwide and perform the vast majority of procedures occurring after the first trimester. Independent clinics are often the last clinics remaining in red states, so these providers are used to seeing patients who have traveled a very long way for care, people who cannot use Medicaid to pay for their abortions, and people who are turned away because they are one day past the gestational limit. These providers know that every day, people are having babies they do not want because they cannot access the abortions they need. The maternal mortality rate in the United States is the highest in the developed world, and in some places that rate is four times as high for black women as for white women. Lack of abortion access is a public health crisis. Eliminating abortion access for poor folks is an instrument of class and racial warfare. When reproductive freedom becomes a class privilege, the human rights of our political body are negated.

The truth of abortion is that people need abortions and always will. You cannot legislate abortion out of existence—you can control only who has safe abortions and who has dangerous ones, who is considered a full person in the eyes of her government and who is a state-owned incubator, who is free and who is not. The Emma Goldman Clinic exists because pregnant people in anti-choice, pro-Trump Iowa are having abortions, all the time. The most insidious anti-choice lie of all is that abortion is partisan. It's not. The kind of person who has an abortion is "everyone." People have abortions across party lines, geographic lines, religious lines, class lines, racial lines. People of all genders have abortions. Rural people have abortions. People of faith have abortions. Anti-choice people have abortions. And you know what? We are fighting for them, too. Part of the way we do that is to simply exist as our whole selves in public, unapologetically.

The chasm between who people claim to be and how they actually behave is vast. We have to fill that chasm up with truth so we can climb out of it.

Silence is not an option. This is not a debate. We cannot go backward. We know that about a third of women have abortions and a majority of Americans support abortion rights in the abstract, even if they are currently inept at talking about it. If we can no longer rely on our political system to protect our rights, all we can do is double down on culture change. We write our stories down, we meet, we talk, we make art, we travel to the places where access is most in jeopardy and we listen, we reach out to our relatives, we hold the line, we chip away. I have been proud to watch Shout Your Abortion flourish into a full-fledged movement: speak-outs, comedy shows, national tours, public art projects, an ever-expanding website flush with every kind of abortion story, a YouTube channel, fashion spreads, a zine of thank-you letters to abortion care providers, a coffee-table book overflowing with truth. SYA is helping people who have had abortions show up and tell the truth about their own lives everywhere. And SYA is just one in a whole network of abortion storytelling campaigns, fighting for truth while the stalwarts on the front lines—led by women of color, as has been the case in every major movement for human rights this country has ever seen—keep doing their work, one day after the next.

Personal storytelling is an engine of humanization, which is in turn an engine of empathy. This is a long game, but if we can change enough minds, voter suppression will lose its power, gerrymandering will be pointless, the electoral college can't stop us. If we unleash our stories, destroy the stigma, and manage to create a broad base of unequivocal cultural support for abortion—the foundation of which is already there—then by the time the more ghastly consequences of abortion bans begin to creep up on politicians, we will have the communication tools to act as an enraged critical mass.

Our stories are ours just as our country is ours just as our bodies are ours.

Leave Hell to the Devils

Sometimes people are surprised to learn that I play video games. And I mean console games, where you're an elf with a fine halberd that you looted from a corpse and you run around stabbing ghouls and picking up, like, eighty-seven of one type of leaf so you can brew a potion that makes you immune to bees, and finishing it takes 120 hours. I play the kind of game where you amass so many longswords that you have to keep fast-traveling back to the bawdy tavern where you keep your trunk so you can free up enough inventory weight that you don't crush your horse, Poop Dumper (I play the kind of games where you get to name your horse).

I've always played video games, on and off—eight-bit Nintendo as a child, PC adventure games with my dad, Final Fantasy in the college dorm, city building on my laptop in my first apartment, Double Dash on the GameCube with my midtwenties roommates, Dragon Age: Inquisition in the early morning before the kids wake up, Zelda: Breath of the Wild when I'm on the road. As I get older, as life gets more complex and the future of the planet grows more uncertain, I find that I increasingly value this escape to a closed, fixable universe. I can't solve the world's problems or even my own tomorrow, but I can help a village seize its croplands back from a restless dead bride.

That said, it has never occurred to me to call myself a "gamer," mainly because I'm not especially good at video games (I play on easy mode—I am scared of monsters!) and I sometimes go months or years without playing them. But also because there's heavy gatekeeping around the term and baggage attached to those who do pick it up. Whether or not girls play video games—and more specifically whether we are qualified to have opinions about them—has become a major culture war fixation over the past decade, uniting aggrieved male gamers against a common enemy that just so happens to look exactly like their moms, mean teachers, all the girls who have ever rejected them, and Hillary Clinton.

The thought of explaining Gamergate to you right now makes my brain want to leave my body and fly into the sun, but I think I can make it through the Cliff's Notes: In 2014, one man was mad at one woman, his ex, who happened to be an indie video game developer. He knew that lots of men and boys around the world were also mad at lots of other women and girls for reasons that maybe they couldn't fully articulate—but which essentially boiled down to the very mild, hard-won shifts away from traditional gender roles that activists had fought for over the past fifty years (aka since America Was Great—this comes back later, unfortunately). The angry man wrote a blog post telling the other men and boys that his ex was the worst kind of New Woman—that she had sex, but not with him anymore, and that she had the gall to make video games, a *boy's* dream! He suggested that any success his ex enjoyed was due not to her talent but to "political correctness" and "fourth-wave feminism," which allowed her to beguile horny, venal male gamers and video games journalists using her sex body. The lesson was quickly drawn by other angry men: other bad women were doing this, too—a whole wave of them!—while also forcing the games journalists to say that game studios should take all the sexy tits out of the video games. Therefore, ruthlessly stalking and harassing women in video games was a truly noble crusade, the only way to save future editions of the Grand Theft Auto franchise from having slightly fewer sex workers you could beat to death. Plus, harassing women online was fun. And so they did.

From there, it was easy for other groups of aggrieved men, those with bigger political agendas, to perk up and come calling. Oh, you feel oppressed by women? Have you heard about the men's rights movement? Oh, you think that calls for diversity in games constitute censorship? You might enjoy this Ben Shapiro fellow or perhaps even this overt white nationalism. Oh, you want a return to traditional values, a time when women knew their place? You might enjoy this presidential candidate named Donald J. Trump.

Mike Cernovich was just a garden-variety men's rights advocate/pickup artist hawking cold-shower virility mumbo jumbo to lonely boys when he made a YouTube video about me, offering—in my recollection—$10,000 to go live with him in Las Vegas for three months so he could prove that he could make any fatty thin through, I assume, gorilla powder and verbal abuse. (The video has since been taken down, a profound loss for anyone who loves making fun of Mike Cernovich, a gain for everyone else.) The goal of the video was to signal to his proto-incel followers that he had lots of money and was a Very Good Troll Boy, and perhaps that worked, but to any remotely well-adjusted adult watching, it was impossible not to read the sputtering, stammering, countertenor tragedy of a man—falling over his words, breathless with excitement at his own joke, and desperate for validation from extremely online virgins—as anything but what he was: a lonely dork begging to pay a woman to be his friend. Needless to say, I declined the offer.

In 2014, Cernovich popped up on my radar again, this time having smelled an opportunity to shepherd and radicalize the Gamergate horde, rebranding himself as a passionate crusader for ethics in video games journalism in order to lead teenage boys to white supremacy and fascism. And it worked! In 2016, he was a driving force behind the troll-built conspiracy theory Pizzagate, which posited that Hillary Clinton and John Podesta were running a child sex ring out of a DC pizza parlor, culminating in the gullible Trumpist idiot Edgar Maddison Welch almost murdering a bunch of people with an assault rifle while they were just trying to chow some 'za. As you probably know, Donald Trump was then elected president (or, as my husband and I call it, "The Incident"), and in 2017, Cernovich was photographed at the White House giving the alt-right "okay" hand sign, which, two years later, the New Zealand mosque shooter, who was radicalized online much like so many Gamergate boys, would flash at his first hearing for murdering fifty peaceful Muslim worshippers.

To put it into internet parlance:

Life!

Comes!

At!

You!

Fast!

By early 2017, I had tweeted thousands of times, maybe tens of thousands. Riffed my beautiful life away. Saw a typoed joke go viral and died inside. Giddily screen grabbed a follow from a hero. Stuck around long enough to see all heroes turn out to be pieces of shit. Was trolled in previously unimaginable ways that soon became all too manageable. And then I quit.

I deactivated my account shortly after President-elect Donald Trump tweeted, "North Korea just stated that it is in the final stages of developing a nuclear weapon capable of reaching parts of the U.S. It won't happen!" on January 2, 2017. I wrote in *The Guardian* that day:

> I deactivated my Twitter account today. It was more of a spontaneous impulse than a New Year resolution, although it does feel like a juice cleanse, a moulting, a polar-bear plunge, a clean slate (except the opposite—like throwing your slate into a volcano and running). One moment I was brains-deep in the usual way, half-heartedly arguing with strangers about whether or not it's "OK" to suggest to Steve Martin that calling Carrie Fisher a "beautiful creature" who "turned out" to be "witty and bright as well" veered just a hair beyond Fisher's stated boundaries regarding objectification (if you have opinions on this, don't tweet me—oh, wait, you can't); and the next moment the US president-elect was using the selfsame platform to taunt North Korea about the size and tumescence of its nuclear program. And I

realised: eh, I'm done. I could be swimming right now. Or flossing. Or digging a big, pointless pit. Anything else.

The North Korea tweet struck me as an unsettling portent of how Trump's presidency was likely to unfold: rash, petty, ostentatiously uninformed, with no regard for public safety or the mechanics of governance. The internet makes neighbors of us all, and my conscience demanded that I put some virtual real estate between myself and the befuddled, racist mobster who was seemingly determined to dismantle and loot the republic. If seeding nuclear war wasn't a violation of Twitter's terms of service, Twitter wasn't a service I wanted to endorse.

Exactly one year later, on January 2, 2018, President Trump tweeted, "North Korean Leader Kim Jong Un just stated that the 'Nuclear Button is on his desk at all times.' Will someone from his depleted and food starved regime please inform him that I too have a Nuclear Button, but it is a much bigger & more powerful one than his, and my Button works!"

How exquisite it would have been to be wrong.

People tend to misconstrue my relationship with internet trolls. They say that trolls hounded me off Twitter (no, it was literally the president, see above) or that I "stalked" and "doxxed" the troll I interviewed for a story that aired on *This American Life* (no, he emailed me) or that I'm obsessed with trolls because they hurt my feelings (no, it's because they were foot soldiers in the fall of American democracy, a slide into fascism that black, trans, and feminist activists detected a decade before any of the white male leftists currently making millions off their self-congratulatory skewering of the alt-right were even paying attention).

It's too late to do anything about that last thing, because none of you fucking listened the first thousand times we mentioned it, and now a Twitter troll is president of the United fucking States, and Twitter CEO Jack Dorsey is complicit in what appear to be multiple percolating genocides as well as the imminent collapse of the planet itself (which, sorry, Nazis, includes white genocide, too!). But, hey, don't feed the trolls. Ignore them and they'll go away! You'll only encourage them by acknowledging their corrosive impact on human interaction and taking steps to discredit and deplatform them!

I keep vowing to never write about internet trolls again, but unfortunately my country's hard dick for ignoring the screams of the marginalized has made internet trolls not just culturally relevant or politically relevant but historically relevant. So here I am—one more troll chapter.

For example, this morning, the president of the United States, angry about actor Alec Baldwin's unflattering portrayal of him on *Saturday Night Live* last night, tweeted, "THE RIGGED AND CORRUPT MEDIA IS THE

ENEMY OF THE PEOPLE!" And that's just today, a random day, a Sunday, the day I decided to sit down and write this chapter I shouldn't have to write. But it could have been any day. Today, though, Donald J. Trump, who is *the president* (?), also tweeted a call for some sort of criminal (??) investigation into Lorne Michaels's long-running NBC comedy variety show, notorious for such chilling Marxist propaganda as "Dick in a Box," "Oops, I Crapped My Pants," and "Mr. Peepers," a recurring sketch in which Chris Kattan plays a sexual monkey who snatches apples (the means of production) from Will Ferrell (Tsar Nicholas II) and gobbles them violently in the faces of various repulsed celebrities (the bourgeoisie). What budding comrade could resist such seductive satirical sweetmeats?

SNL's assault on democracy this week came in the form of a cold open in which Mr. Baldwin lampooned a recent White House press conference on the newly declared state of emergency, dealing grave insult to Mr. Trump by, essentially, quoting him accurately about his idiot wall. "I want wall!" Baldwin-as-Trump bleats again and again, "Wall keep safe!" It's a cogent and efficient summary of the last two years of Trumpist policy: weaponized xenophobic nonsense battered relentlessly against our skulls until everyone is dead (jk, we wish) and then Trump goes golfing. Somewhere, a glacier calves.

I am writing this chapter, against my will, because people still love to scoff at the significance of Twitter and its culture of abuse. It's "just" social media. Tweets are "just" tweets. I pale at the need to explain this, but "just" tweets such as "THE RIGGED AND CORRUPT MEDIA IS THE ENEMY OF THE PEOPLE!," when tweeted by the president, actually matter quite a bit, because Trump's endgame, communications-wise, is to silo his supporters to the point that he is literally their only trusted source of news, opinion, and truth—and Twitter is the platform on which he talks to them. It matters.

The Republican Party long ago ceased any limp gestures toward holding Trump accountable for anything, and Fox News (minus Shep) never even went through the motions. The Democrat-controlled House has been cock-blocking Trump in some satisfying ways, but it's only one branch of our big, sick government. Trump has been stacking the lower courts with servile bootlickers, and with Brett Kavanaugh and Neil Gorsuch on the Supreme Court, he has effectively hamstrung progress for decades even if he himself is impeached tomorrow.

The media are our last independent check on Trump's authority—and, especially, his lies—lies he disseminates using Twitter, the same platform he uses to try to destroy the press. In the past week, the president tweeted a promise of a new North Korea: "North Korea will become a different kind of Rocket - an Economic one!"; he has assured his followers that "the Wall is being built and will be a great achievement and contributor toward life and safety within our Country!"; and he let everyone know that; "No president ever worked harder than me (cleaning up the mess I inherited)!"

It's a strategy I recognize: telling people the lies they're hungry for, constructing an alternate reality, refusing to back down in the face of facts, spamming the discursive field until people just accept that it must have some legitimacy in the "debate"—Trumpism is the internet troll playbook.

Is it any wonder, after years of being told "Don't feed the trolls," American society has no idea whatsoever how to deal with Trumpism? The necessary response is social ostracism. The necessary response is to set firm institutional boundaries. The necessary response is not to reopen closed debates. The necessary response is to block and report, and by report I mean *say the truth, over and over, until it sticks.*

Instead—on Twitter and in Trump's America—most people just sit, bewildered, on the high road and try to get on with their lives. It doesn't work. I promise.

When you work in media, Twitter becomes part of your job. It's where you orient yourself in "the discourse"—figure out what's going on, what people are saying about it, and, more important, what no one has said yet. In a lucky coup for Twitter's marketing team, prevailing wisdom among media types has long held that quitting the platform could be a career killer. The illusion that Twitter visibility and professional relevance are indisputably inextricable always felt too risky to puncture.

Who could afford to call that bluff and be wrong? So we stayed, while Twitter's endemic racist, sexist, and transphobic harassment problems grew increasingly more sophisticated and organized.

Being on Twitter felt like being in a nonconsensual BDSM relationship with the apocalypse. So I left. I wrote jokes there for free. I posted political commentary for free. I answered questions for free. I taught Feminism 101 for free. Off Twitter, these are all things by which I make my living—in fact, they make up the totality of my income. But on Twitter, I did them pro bono, and in return, I was micromanaged in real time by strangers; neo-Nazis mined my personal life for vulnerabilities to exploit; and men enjoyed unfettered, direct access to my brain so they could inform me, for the thousandth time, that they would gladly rape me if I weren't so fat.

I talked back, and I was "feeding the trolls." I said nothing, and the harassment escalated. I reported threats, and I was a "censor." I used mass blocking tools to curb abuse, and I was abused further for blocking "unfairly." I had to conclude, after half a decade of workshopping, that it may simply be impossible to make this platform usable for anyone but trolls, robots, and dictators.

Those of us who complained about online abuse were consistently told—by colleagues, armchair experts, and random internet strangers—that we were the problem. We were too soft. We, who literally inured ourselves to rape threats and death threats so that we could participate in public life, were called weak by people who felt persecuted by the existence of female Ghostbusters. Meanwhile, Twitter's leadership offered us the ability to embed GIFs.

Those of us who pointed out that online harassment was politically motivated—compounded by race, gender, and sexual orientation—as I did in 2013, for example, were accused of being "professional victims" trying to leverage our paranoid delusions to censor the internet. That defamation has never been retracted or atoned for even after the revelations that an army of Russian Twitter bots functions as the Trump administration's propaganda wing and the alt-right, essentially a coalition of antifeminist, white supremacist online harassment campaigns, recruits angry young men to Trumpism by framing the abuse of social justice activists as a team sport. Meanwhile, Twitter's leadership offered us 280 characters.

The social contract of the internet seems to insist that there's nobility in weathering degradation. You can call me oversensitive, but the truth is, I got far better than any human being should have to at absorbing astonishing cruelty and feeling nothing. Undersensitivity was just another piece of workplace safety gear.

In 2012, out of morbid curiosity, I clicked on the home page of a stranger who had been saying aggressive, repulsive things to me on Twitter and found my way to his personal YouTube channel. I was relatively new to blogging on a national platform and struggling to get my bearings in the thick of my first large-scale hate mob—hundreds of people flooding my social media feeds with cruel, frightening messages—in retaliation for what, exactly, I can't even remember. I'd written something that some men didn't like, and they felt the need, en masse, to shut me up. As a fat feminist, it happens to me all the time.

To my surprise, the man used his full name and didn't hide his face (most of my harassers stay meticulously anonymous). Even more unusually, his videos betrayed genuine vulnerability. He was the platonic form of an internet troll: bald, goateed, bespectacled, and doughy, fighting a stammer, broadcasting from a dreary, dark room. And he was sad. "I'm making this vlog because I am not happy with the direction my life is going," he mumbled in a soft, high-pitched voice. "I don't like my career, if you can call it that, I'm unhappy with the way that I look, I am not satisfied with myself as a man, and not just as a man but as a human being."

Oh, I realized. Internet trolls have bad lives. Happy people don't do this.

I don't want horrible men to be doxxed and threatened online; I want them to be better. I want women to be able to fight for gender equality (or even just relay our lived experiences) without having to face years of libel, stalking, emotional labor, howling rage, and relentless degradation. I want feminists to be able to do our work. I want my daughters to be safe. I want men to understand that women's sexual boundaries are not a gray area and women's time and attention are not public commodities. I want men who feel frustrated and invisible, all those sad men in dark rooms, to find fulfillment in communities that don't leverage female dehumanization for male validation.

You know what actually got them to leave me alone? Quitting Twitter. Refusing to play. Essentially, deplatforming them from my life. It works. The tech companies allowing white supremacy and violent misogyny to flourish on their platforms could do something about it. Never forget that they *choose* not to.

In December 2016, Twitter CEO Jack Dorsey tweeted, "What's the most important thing you want to see Twitter improve or create in 2017?" One user responded, "Comprehensive plan for getting rid of the Nazis."

"We've been working on our policies and controls," Dorsey replied. "What's the next most critical thing?" Oh, what's our second highest priority after Nazis? I'd say number two is also Nazis. And number three. In fact, you can just go ahead and slide "Nazis" into the top one hundred spots. Get back to me when your website isn't a roiling rat king of Nazis. Nazis are bad, you see?

Trump uses his Twitter account to set hate mobs on private citizens, attempt to silence journalists who write unfavorably about him, lie to the American people, and bulldoze complex diplomatic relationships with other world powers. I quit Twitter because it felt unconscionable to be a part of it—to generate revenue for it, participate in its profoundly broken culture, and lend my name to its legitimacy. Twitter is home to a wealth of powerful anti-Trump organizing, as well, but I'm personally weary of feeling hostage to a platform that has treated me and the people I care about so poorly. We can do good work elsewhere.

I'm pretty sure that "ushered in kleptocracy" would be a deal breaker for any other company that wanted my business. If my gynecologist regularly hosted neo-Nazi rallies in the exam room, I would find someone else to swab my cervix. If I found out my favorite coffee shop was even remotely complicit in the third world war, I would—bare minimum—switch coffee shops; I might give up coffee altogether.

We need systemic change, not whack-a-mole with one grandiose troll at a time. But change has been so slow, mystifyingly slow, even while the troll in the White House tweets threats and typos and personal attacks on individual citizens. In April 2019, Dorsey met with Trump in the Oval Office to reassure the president that Twitter was not artificially lowering his follower count. A month later, Twitter announced that it is launching—and remember, *this is motherfucking May 2019*—an in-house research project to START to TRY to figure out whether or not it is good to let white supremacists organize and radicalize others on their platform. "Is it the right approach to deplatform these individuals?" a Twitter executive told Vice. "Is the right approach to try and engage with these individuals? How should we be thinking about this? What actually works?"

It's farcical. It's literally a farce. Here's an idea: maybe instead of trying to troubleshoot the Nazi factory inside a clown's asshole, we just let it go.

It wasn't brave to quit Twitter or righteous or noteworthy. Quitting Twitter is just a thing you can do. I mention it only because there was a time when I didn't think it was a thing I could do, and then I did it, and now my life is better.

I'm frequently approached by colleagues, usually women, who ask me about quitting Twitter with hushed titillation, as if I've escaped a cult or broken a particularly seductive taboo. Here's what my Twitter-free life is like: I don't wake up with a pit in my stomach every day, dreading what horrors accrued in my phone overnight. I don't get dragged into protracted, bad-faith arguments with teenage boys about whether poor people deserve medical care or whether putting nice guys into the friend zone is a hate crime. I don't spend hours every week blocking and reporting trolls and screen grabbing abuse in case it someday escalates into a credible threat. I no longer feel as though my brain is trapped in a centrifuge filled with swastikas and Alex Jones's spittle. Time is finite, and now I have more of it.

At the same time, I know this conversation is more complicated than that. I've lost a large platform to promote my work and make professional connections, which isn't something many writers can afford to give up (less established writers and marginalized writers most of all—in a horrid irony, the same writers who are disproportionately abused on Twitter). I get my news on a slight delay. I seethe at the perception that I ceded any ground to trolls who were trying to push me out. I will probably never persuade RuPaul to be my friend. Also, I loved Twitter. Twitter is funny and smart and validating and cathartic. It feels, when you are embroiled in it, like the place where everything is happening. The president of the United States makes major policy announcements there. This is the world now.

I shouldn't have had to walk away from all that because for Twitter to take a firm stance against neo-Nazism might have cost it some incalculable sliver of profit. No one should. As in everything, global culture change would have been better. But I didn't have global culture change, and I'm better equipped to fight for global culture change now that I'm not trapped in an eternal siege by a sea of angry boy-men, an unknown percentage of whom are probably robots.

When you deactivate a verified Twitter account (nail polish emoji), you have one year to log back in or your account—everything you ever tweeted, every reply in every thread—is permanently deleted. I always planned to log in and then immediately deactivate again, to re-up for another year. I figured I'd eventually reactivate, even if just for posterity. I was part of some important cultural conversations; I had said some smart things before other people said them; I had made some good jokes. One time the actor Michael McKean called me "doodlebug" in an affectionate manner because he liked one of my movie reviews. I wouldn't have minded preserving that.

But in January 2018, I realized: it was too late. I'd forgotten to log back in. More than a year had passed. It was all gone. It's as though a great wind came and blew my problem novel into the river. It's as though I ate a very good sandwich without taking a picture of it. Sometimes it is okay to just let things go.

Anger Is a Weapon

I did not call myself a feminist until I was nearly twenty years old. My world had taught me that feminists were ugly, angry, and ridiculous, and I did not want to be ugly, angry, and ridiculous. I wanted to be cool and desired by men, because even as a teenager I knew implicitly that pandering for male approval was what women were supposed to do. It was my best shot at success, or at least safety, and I wasn't sophisticated enough to see that success and safety, bestowed conditionally, aren't success and safety at all; they are domestication and implied violence.

To put it another way, it took me two decades to become brave enough to be angry.

In October 2017, as the full horror of what Harvey Weinstein had done came into public view, an *Access Hollywood* correspondent asked the actress Uma Thurman to comment on abuse of power in Hollywood, presumably in light of the sexual assault allegations against Weinstein.

Speaking slowly and deliberately, through gritted teeth, Thurman responded, "I don't have a tidy sound bite for you, because I've learned—I am not a child—and I have learned that when I've spoken in anger I usually regret the way I express myself. So I've been waiting to feel less angry. And when I'm ready, I'll say what I have to say."

Thurman was seething, as we have all been seething, in our various states of breaking open or, as Thurman chose, waiting. It took her a few more months until she decided she was ready, and at last she explained how even at the height of her fame, making money for Weinstein as his cool girl star, he had gone after her, too.

Women are seething at how long we have been ignored, seething for the ones who were long ago punished for telling the truth, seething for being told all of our lives that we have no right to seethe. Thurman's rage was palpable yet contained, conveying not just the tempestuous depths of #MeToo but a profound understanding of the ways in which female anger is received and weaponized against women.

There is a woman who became a meme. In 2013, she went to a protest, and a clip of her anger went viral. The stalking and harassment she has endured since are on a scale beyond comprehension. She was participating in a protest against a men's rights group, proponents of a male supremacist movement that the Southern Poverty Law Center describes as "a hateful ideology advocating for the subjugation of women."

The men's rights movement (which fed directly into the alt-right) was in itself an elaborate troll, preying on disaffected young men's resentments and insecurities to entice them to join what was framed as a social justice movement, then deploying them to make women's lives hell both online and off. They did not fight for paid paternal leave, raise money to build domestic violence shelters for men, or encourage men to go to therapy and learn to be vulnerable and share their feelings instead of seeking cruel catharsis in degrading and abusing women. Instead, they spent their time doing things like flooding Occidental College's online rape reporting tool with false rape reports. Or advocating for the legalization of rape on private property. Or declaring "Bash a Violent Bitch Month" in protest against women, supposedly, being allowed to beat their male partners with impunity. Or, mainly, just writing lots and lots of blog posts about how women are bad and harassing lots and lots of women on Twitter.

It was a movement designed to make women angry, so that men could take that anger and hold it up and say, "See? See? They *are* hysterical. They *are* violent. They *do* hate men."

That's what they did to the woman who became a meme. She was angry that day—and why shouldn't she have been?—attempting to read a statement, her voice rising to compete with the crowd, and when she was interrupted she would stop and say something such as "Can you shut the fuck up for a second, so I can read my fucking list?" In keeping with their model, one of the men's rights advocates filmed her and uploaded the video to YouTube. What followed was six years (and counting) of threats, abuse, mockery, and privacy violations. She became the face of vicious feminist hysteria, her image replicated and caricatured over and over and over, ceaselessly, on Twitter and Facebook and YouTube and the damp underbelly of every fetid "manosphere" message board. The revered evolutionary biologist Richard Dawkins tweeted a video in which a grotesque caricature of the woman (a real person) encourages a grotesque caricature of a Muslim man to rape her, a nod to one of the online Right's favorite tropes—that supposedly PC feminists shrug at sexual assault when it's committed by Muslims, because to accuse them of rape would be Islamophobic.

Interestingly, the statement that the woman was trying to read in the video that would eat her life wasn't actually particularly angry at all. I know because I wrote it.

She was reading from an article I had written in *Jezebel* in 2013 called "If I Admit That 'Hating Men' Is a Thing, Will You Stop Turning It Into a Self-Fulfilling Prophecy?" The point of that piece was that feminists are already doing many of the things that men's rights activists claim to be fighting for. Their anger is not at cross-purposes.

But it didn't matter what she was saying. None of it was ever about communication, a good-faith exchange of ideas.

It was about making women mad so you can call them crazy and justify hurting them to make yourself feel better about your broken little life and cling to your pitiful scraps of institutional power because you have no power as a person.

In April 2016, more than three years after the protest, the woman was shopping at a state-run liquor store when an employee recognized her from his antifeminist internet circles. *National Post* reported that the employee then downloaded security camera footage of her and posted it on social media.

This is what the (government!) employee's Facebook post said:

> I helped her select something for about 5 minutes, some guy interrupted us and I fully expected her to go off on a rant but it appears that she's selective about when to explode. And now I can safely say that after speaking with [REDACTED] that I work with a woman more unstable than her. I deliberately asked her if she needed help to confirm her voice, and my God everything checks out.

She was just shopping in a liquor store—buying tequila for margarita Monday, maybe, or a retirement gift for Bob in sales who loves Scotch—a full three years after losing her temper one time, and a person purporting to help her pick the right bottle, who is paid by her tax dollars, lay in wait. He "helped her select something," he expected her to "rant" while being interrupted. She surprised him by not being as "unstable" as he expected, almost as though her individual personhood had been deliberately flattened into a meme to justify discrediting and abusing not just her but women as a whole. Almost!

His post led people "to suggest they should search for her in the suburb West of Toronto in order to sexually assault her," *National Post* reported.

By July, when she went to the press with the story, the woman said that she still did not know whether the employee had been fired and that local police had not followed up on her complaint. "They refuse to communicate with me, and all I want to know is did this guy get fired and should I prepare for any kind of retaliation," she said.

In the story, the government official who oversees the liquor board said he thought the retailer would figure out what had happened but that he condemned all forms of harassment. He "pointed to the government strategy to combat sexual violence: *It's Never Ok.*"

"It's Never Ok."

In the fall of 2018, the world saw that actually, sometimes, it seems like it is okay.

At the confirmation hearings for Justice Brett Kavanaugh, Christine Blasey Ford told the House Judiciary Committee, and everyone else, about what she remembered happening to her when she was fifteen and Kavanaugh was seventeen and they were both in the suburban Maryland high school world of drinking, parties, and meticulously up-to-date teenage datebooks.

Ford told lawmakers that on a summer evening at a party in Montgomery County, Kavanaugh had forced her onto a bed, groped her, tried to pull off her clothing and bathing suit, and put his hand over her mouth.

"I thought he might inadvertently kill me," she said when she spoke publicly for the first time, to the *Washington Post.*

On the day of the extra hearing to go over the allegations, Kavanaugh was angry. He wasn't seething, he was shouting. Indignant. Spittle flying, frustrated tears welling up in his small black eyes. He felt no need to suppress his anger—his anger, by the way, not at being sexually assaulted but at being credibly accused of sexual assault.

Blasey's testimony was achingly, supernaturally poised. She was so, so careful. The microphone wasn't quite where it was supposed to be.

"I'll lean forward," she said. "Is this good?"

Am I doing it right? I am not angry.

Blasey let herself be grilled in front of the entire nation—reliving a moment when she thought she might be raped or killed—to save us. She put her body in between Kavanaugh and the Supreme Court, Kavanaugh and *Roe v. Wade*, Kavanaugh and what he wanted. She stayed serene for us, and she was perfect for us.

He won. She was nice, and she lost.

Ford was still receiving threats and harassment months after the hearing. She was forced to move four times for her safety. She had to pay for private guards and has not yet returned to her professorship at Palo Alto University. She essentially lives in hiding.

Brett Kavanaugh is on the Supreme Court.

If we lose either way, why the fuck shouldn't we just let our anger out?

Is there a woman who has lost her temper in public and didn't face ridicule, temporary ruin, or both? Can you think of one? Solange? Britney Spears? Sinéad O'Connor? The Dixie Chicks? Rosie O'Donnell?

Women are supposed to be compliant and helpful and nice and play the support role for men who are the real actors in the world. We are supposed to absorb, not project.

We don't even have to be angry to be called angry—that's the power of stigma. Accusations of being an "angry black woman" chased Michelle Obama throughout her tenure at the White House, despite eight years of unflappable poise (black women suffer disproportionately under this paradigm). The decades-long smearing of Hillary Clinton as an unhinged shrew culminated in November 2016 when, despite maintaining a preternatural calm throughout the most brutal campaign in living memory, she lost the election to apoplectic masculinity itself.

Like every other feminist with a public platform, I am perpetually cast as a disapproving scold.

But what's the alternative? To approve? I do not approve.

Not only are women expected to weather sexual violence, intimate partner violence, workplace discrimination, institutional subordination, the expectation of free domestic labor, the blame for our own victimization, and all the subtler, invisible cuts that undermine us daily, we are not even allowed to be angry about it.

We are expected to keep quiet about the men who prey upon us, as though their predation was our choice, not theirs. We are expected to sit quietly as men debate whether or not the state should be allowed to forcibly use our bodies as incubators. They call us "hosts" and then apologize clumsily, and we are supposed to say thank you? We are expected not to complain as we are diminished, degraded, and discredited.

We are expected to agree (and we comply!) with the paternal admonition that it is irresponsible and hyperemotional to request one female president after centuries of male ones—because that would be tokenism, antidemocratic and dangerous—as though generations of white male politicians haven't proven themselves utterly uninterested in caring for the needs of communities to which they do not belong. As though white men's monopolistic death grip on power in the United States doesn't belie precisely the kind of "identity politics" they claim to abhor. As though competent, qualified women are so thin on the ground that even a concerted, sincere, large-scale search for one would be a long shot and any resulting candidate a compromise.

When, finally, an inspiring group of women is running for president, we are told to still wring our hands over who is likable, who is feminist enough, who is too feminist, or if nominating a woman is a risk worth taking when the alternative is more Donald Trump. Let's take another look at Uncle Joe.

When a woman gets angry, the typical response is: She didn't understand what happened. She misunderstood. She's bleeding out of her whatever. She shouldn't have taken all that sexual harassment, or her boss's hand on her ass, so personally. It was just mixed signals! Locker room talk! She shouldn't blow it out of proportion. He was raised in a different time—nothing to be angry about. But what was that different time when being treated with zero bodily autonomy was nothing to be angry about, as if all our fathers and grandfathers were sexual predators? They weren't. Men can choose how they treat us, and this is the world they choose. Frankly, not being angry would be irrational.

Feminism is the collective manifestation of female anger.

Men suppress our anger for a reason. Let's prove them right.

Magic Isn't Magic

Not to brag, but in 2015 I wrote a memoir called *Shrill*, and in 2016 Elizabeth Banks optioned it for television, and in 2017 Aidy Bryant signed on to play me, and in 2018 we actually wrote and shot *Shrill*, the show, a body-positive half-hour comedy by Hulu (STREAMING NOW!!!!) . . . and psych, suckers, *yes to brag*!! But only because this is a very wild thing to happen to a person and an exceedingly unlikely thing to happen at all (especially to me, an only quasisentient body pillow who DVRs *Guy's Grocery Games* and whose favorite Dorito flavor is Spicy Sweet Chili—*what*!?), so it would almost be disrespectful *not* to brag about it, if you think about it.

Plus, women are conditioned from birth to downplay our intellectual abilities and professional accomplishments so as not to make men feel threatened or emasculated by us and detract from our true purpose, sex decoration, which makes bragging about my TV show in a season when many, many men tried to get TV shows and failed, an #act #of #resistance #AND #I #THINK #WE #CAN #ALL #AGREE #VERY #BRAVE. You're welcome!

Four years ago, I had nothing but my brain, which is a cursed jelly (?) inside the top of my body that usually just says "Annihilate Doritos" over and over (unless I am asleep, in which case IT YELLS IT) and also makes sure I hold my pee in, usually. With the help of my productivity guru, Bo (full name Bo Ookadvancethatiwouldvehadto-payback), I managed to tame my skull goo long enough to produce an entire book, and now that book is a full fucking television show and I got to hug Daniel Stern because of it. I turned my brain into Daniel Stern in four years! Me! A straight-B student with both the body type and the complexion of one of those German sausages that look like a sausage's ghost! (They're called *Weisswurst*, by the way, a fact I found by googling "name of the pale sausage," which is also what Lindy means in Dothraki.)

Based on my experiences in Hollywood with Hollywood people, show business is—to quote Benjamin Franklin—99 percent sushi meetings about stuff that will never happen and 1 percent perspiration. Because it's hot in Los Angeles. In fact, it was over 100 degrees when I went for my first meeting with Liz—THAT'S WHAT I CALL HER—Banks, and I was manufacturing a *truly medical* amount of sweat. Liz's waiting area has those spindly Eames molded fiberglass chairs (probably not even knockoffs) that are terrifying to fat people even though they look like dim sum spoons, and, as I waited, my huge wet ass created a perfect suction over the concave bowl of the chair so that when Liz's assistant came to get me it went SSSLLLUUUUURRRRRRP! Which is a great way to start a meeting when you are a fat-ass country mouse begging a movie star to believe in you a millions-of-dollars amount!

But anyway, it worked. So try it, I guess?

The process of writing a television show about your life is strange and in many ways very bad, involving questions such as "Does she fuck him without a condom because she's stupid or because she hates herself?" and "What season should we have the dad die?" I cannot wholeheartedly recommend it, but if nevertheless you persist, be forewarned that a bulk of your time in the writers' room will be spent begging the other writers not to include EVERY single humiliating detail about your ex that will imply you're still thinking about him fifteen years later even though you *dredged up that dead memory only because you needed an example of something really really dumb*!!! (You will fail, and it will all go in there.)

But also, obviously, making *Shrill*, a body-positive half-hour comedy by Hulu streaming now, was one of the most magical, lucky, unreal experiences of my life. Not just because working on a set is very fun (it is) and our crew is a circus of warmhearted geniuses dedicated to excellence in all things (they are!) but because I got to make a real fucking TV show about a fat chick with a personality.

When I was doing press for *Shrill* the book—and even back when I was pitching it, actually—I always told people that I just wanted to write the book that I needed to read when I was 14, 15, 16 . . . 27, 28, 29 . . . 37. A book about a fat character you couldn't help but fall in love with, who had a complex, dynamic life, who had sex and had fun and got to make mistakes that didn't involve cake pops. When I was pitching the show to production companies and then to networks, I always said, "I want to make a show about a fat woman where at no point does she step on a scale, look down, and sigh." I got to make that book, and I got to make that show, and literally every day strangers come up to me on the street and tell me it helped, a little or a lot. It helped me, too. That's an accomplishment. But it's not the solution.

Just squeezing through the very, very, very narrow doors of Hollywood—an infrastructure built in deep, sick ways around conventional white female beauty—feels like a triumph in itself. I am almost always the fattest person at the meeting. Just my presence changes people's understanding of the ambition and capability of fat people. I know that my body in the room changes how people talk, which, eventually, may rewire how some of them think. TV executives and agents and managers and actors nod fervently when I say things like "It's okay to be fat," partly because they really do want to be good, to move into the future, to help, and maybe even to be free, but it's also because body positivity sells now. Buying it is one thing; living it is another. (Here's how you can tell we're still at the starting line, not the finish: body positivity sells best when it's skinny white models selling it.) I know what the Hollywood people eat for lunch, that the men eat more than the women, that when it comes to describing the protagonist of my TV series they contort and spasm before saying the word *fat*, if they can get it out at all. Usually it comes out as "You know . . . uh . . . plus . . . uh . . . b-b-b-b-b-b-b . . . uh . . . b-b-b-b-b-big-bigger . . . ladies [car peeling out]."

Yes, we got a show onto the air. But visibility isn't justice.

Visibility didn't change the fact that when I went to the doctor limping from an ankle injury, she suggested I try "stretching," then let me know that Weight Watchers has an app now. I had to insist on an X-ray, which—after a couple months of limping procrastination on my part (HEY, I HAD A BOOK DUE)—revealed a bone spur stabbing me in my Achilles tendon. "Well, more of a giant bone shelf," the podiatrist later told me. It will probably need surgery. The stretching had made it worse.

Visibility didn't help all the fat people who've died from bariatric surgery complications or whose cancer symptoms were waved away as side effects of "poor lifestyle." Ashley Graham wearing a size 12 on the cover of

Sports Illustrated does jack shit for women who wear a size 36 and have nothing to wear to a wedding tomorrow. Or, God forbid, need a suit for a last-minute job interview, at which they may be considered lazier and less intelligent because of the size of their bodies.

Visibility didn't help me at all the public events I've done where I've walked onstage—*to talk about being fat*—and discovered that the chairs were too narrow. Or all the photo shoots I've showed up to—*to publicize my book or TV show about being fat*—and discovered that none of the clothes fit, even if I'd sent my measurements months in advance. Visibility didn't help me find a dress to wear to the premiere of my TV show about being fat—*which is about being fat*—and it didn't help our wardrobe department find cute, fashion-forward looks for Aidy to wear on the show. They custom-made almost all of her clothes.

Yeah, I'm a witch and I'm hunting you, and so on, but catching you doesn't liberate fat people any more than trapping one fox makes chickens immortal. This kind of witchcraft, unfortunately, isn't magic.

One of the things you are asked to do to promote a television show is attend an event called the TCAs (Television Critics of America), an annual three-week conference during which networks present their new lineups to journalists from across the country. The idea, as I understand it (caveat: I DON'T) is to give critics who don't live in LA or New York "access to talent"—i.e., imprison the staff of the

Cleveland Scene in a hotel for three weeks and beat them about the head and neck with Topher Grace twelve to thirteen hours per day. In 2019, the event was at the Langham Huntington Pasadena, a sprawling daytime soap set where you need a cartographer, a boatswain, *and a boatswain's mate* to find your room, they still have a landline next to the toilet, and dim sum costs fif-tee-hayght-doll-hairs. It is the best place I have ever been.

There were eight of us on the panel to present *Shrill*: Aidy, Liz, me, Ali Rushfield (our show runner), and four cast members: Lolly Adefope, John Cameron Mitchell, Ian Owens, and Luka Jones. Our panel was thirty minutes long (which would be tight for a panel of one person, let alone eight, six of whom are actors), followed by a portion literally called "scrum," during which, TCA handlers explained, the reporters would be allowed to run at us and yell anything they liked. Alluring!

That morning, I flew a little too close to the sun with the snooze button and had to jog to hair and makeup. On the way, I rounded a corner and discovered the pee-drinking survivalist Bear Grylls perched on a mahogany side table like a little wood elf. I tossed him an acorn, and he granted me one wish (A THOUSAND MORE WISHES, BITCH!), and I slid into the greenroom just in time to watch George Clooney eat a breakfast burrito. He looks like shit in person, by the way. Repulsive. A true hog. Dr. Ruth was in the makeup chair next to mine. We held hands. (We didn't.)

The journalists—maybe two hundred of them—sat at long banquet tables in a dim hotel ballroom, clacking away at their laptops. We were warned in advance that the crowd would be "chilly" and not to expect them to laugh at any of our jokes. We took the stage. They did not look up.

The first few questions covered the usual ground—"Why do you choose to use the word *fat*?" "How is the show different from the book?"—and we answered them with as much flair as we could in a largely silent room. Then a certain contingent of journalists took the wheel and steered us off the road and into an ideological culvert from which none of us would ever escape.

I believe the first to broach the topic was a Frenchman in the back. "Uh, Ee-leez-eh-beyth, yeu arh seuh be-yeu-teh-fehll, uh, tell meee, why weuld yeu be drhown teu eh preh-dzhect lehk zees?"

The implication was pretty clear. Elizabeth. You are hot! Why would you give a shit about *zees cochons gros*?

Elizabeth fielded the question with poise and patience, explaining that the book resonated with her for many reasons and that any woman working in Hollywood has to deal with coercive expectations placed on her body. She told a story about her first-ever meeting with a Hollywood agent: "He told me I needed to get a boob job. I did not get a boob job, and I decided that I was going to be happy and comfortable with who I was."

Liz tried to steer the conversation away from her body, talking about her ambitions as a director and her determination to create the kinds of roles for women—telling women's stories—that she'd always wanted to play. Another man had a follow-up question about the boob job.

An older woman raised her hand and essentially rephrased the Frenchman: "But Elizabeth! You're gorgeous! You've always been gorgeous! What could possibly interest you in a story like this?"

Then there were what felt like several more decades of variations on the question of Elizabeth's hot body.

"You know," Liz said eventually, "this was not the most interesting thing to me about this project and Lindy's book." Both the book and the show are about reproductive rights, women's challenges in the workplace, and family, love, and friendship, and we'd actually succeeded in making a relatively radical piece of feminist art and bringing it into the mainstream, and here was a room full of people who *had watched the show*, and all they could think about was how much bigger and less desirable my body and Aidy's body were than Liz's.

Elizabeth Banks is the most successful female director of all time. She's the thirtieth-highest-grossing actor of all time and the ninth-highest-grossing female actor of all time. She runs a company. We had literally just made a show about exactly this kind of monomaniacal reductionism.

Elizabeth, if you had gotten that boob job, would you have played with them? And could you describe what that might have been like?

Elizabeth! It seems odd that you'd choose this project rather than one where a beautiful woman takes doodies on fat people. Could you speak to that?

Then all two hundred journalists rushed the stage to ask Liz questions about *Charlie's Angels.* I spent the rest of the day doing interviews with female journalists, each of whom apologized extravagantly about the latter part of the Q and A. It made me sad when I realized my genuine response: In the moment, those questions had barely even registered. I've been asked worse.

The society this culture created is well fortified. A few creepy men losing their jobs, a few women managing to clamber to the top—those things matter, but they don't actually change how people think and behave on a large scale. Fuck, they don't even change how people think and behave on a small scale *toward those individual men and women.*

The hardest truth to swallow isn't that this cultural moment—the reckoning, the witches are coming, the last straw—is not a finish line but that there may be no finish line at all. Maybe we will have to fight forever. So be it. I have a thousand wishes.

The World Is Good and Worth Fighting For

You know that exquisite love you have for a person or a place? For me it's my husband, Ahamefule, my best friend, vibrating with ideas and brilliantly talented, a talent once in a generation and on the brink of everyone knowing it, wise and principled, who is so annoying, who can lift a piano, who can lift me.

If we are walking from one place to another and we pass anything crotch height—say, a fire hydrant—Ahamefule pretends not to see it, walks right into it, and goes "HOHHHHHHHHHHHH" like it hit him in the nuts. We fight once a year. He is sensitive in the morning, so I am careful not to talk about bills until after 10:00 a.m., which makes for a quiet sort of dawn ritual: we wake up with the sun or because I am snoring, and we lie in bed for as long as we can and we talk about only good stuff.

I also love my place, the Pacific Northwest, Seattle, the Olympic Peninsula, in whatever complex capacity stolen Klallam, Skokomish, and Duwamish land can be "mine." When I am home, I can feel the decades of my mother and father's lives, separate and together, the ground shaped by their feet, my understanding of the city shaped by the old family stories:

Late 1940s, my father, on his paper route in Madrona, when there's an earthquake and a woman runs into the street, fully nude from the bath, screaming.

Early 1960s, my mother, second youngest of seven, flying out the door of their sardine-packed house at 55th and 12th, racing south on Roosevelt for some private peace at the library that's still there on 50th. A decade later, same neighborhood, she's living alone, long blond hair, and Ted Bundy murders a girl down the block in that cruel way men can take your streets from you.

Early 1950s, my father living in a storefront on 34th Ave S—it's the Hi Spot now—with a pack of young dudes; he plays piano in a cocktail lounge downtown seven nights a week. Mid-1970s, my mother standing on top of Mount St. Helens, which she climbed, a summit that doesn't exist anymore, a place that's gone—or it's dust and vapor now, maybe some of it is in Japan, some in Egypt, some still sifting down through the Atlantic. Same era, my father, husky, big black beard, leather briefcase, commuting on the ferry from Bainbridge Island, striding up Columbia or

Cherry or James to the ad agency, wherever it was, probably greeting every person he passed; he knew everyone, and the city was small.

My dad is gone now and so is that Seattle, but walking in the places he walked, puffing up the same hills, turning the same corners, I feel him in the ridges and grooves of my city—we are close, superimposed, separated only by time, and what's that? This is the only religion that I can relate to.

The Northwest is a layered place. May through September: blue water, green trees, white mountains, blue sky. October through April: gray water, gray trees, white mountains, gray sky. I remember coming home from college in Los Angeles and taking the ferry across Puget Sound, watching the land sitting long, low, and dark on the water. I looked at it, and for the first time I didn't think, "This is my home," but instead "This is my habitat," as though if you put me somewhere else I would fade and die. A polar bear trying to be a flamingo.

I remember the first summer all the snow melted in the mountains. Blue water, green trees, brown mountains, blue sky. It was just a few years ago. Now it's every summer.

One early August day in 2017, I looked at the weather forecast and it read "89 degrees, smoke."

The sky turned brown and opaque. The neighboring city of Bellevue, which normally glitters above Lake Washington to the east, disappeared. The mountains disappeared. I didn't see a tree move for an entire week. It was like a giant cloche had been placed over the whole region, as though God were playing molecular gastronomy and we were her smoked langoustine cotton candy duck balloons. You could feel the air on your skin, powdery and wrong, somehow both sweltering and clammy. Residents were warned not to exercise; people with asthma clutched their inhalers, white knuckled.

To live in Seattle is to exist, perpetually, in the bargaining stage of grief. From October through May, generally speaking, it drizzles. Every day. What gets us through the gray, like a mantra, is the promise of summer. Summers in Seattle are perfect, bright blue and fresh, and all winter long we assure ourselves, over and over, "This is worth it for that." Please let this one be a good summer, a long summer, a real Seattle summer. We need it. It's our medicine.

The smoke stole our summer, as it would the summer after. People were on edge. One day in the car, my husband was telling me about two guys he saw fighting on the street, and I got distracted by two guys fighting on the street.

I can't say definitively that our now-annual, unprecedented wildfires are the direct result of human-made climate change. I am not a scientist. But those smoke-choked months have thrown formerly intangible feelings of dread into stark perspective. While the smoke hovered, I remember staring at the low, dirty sky and thinking "What if this never left? What if it got worse?"

I do know that the planet is getting warmer, that Donald Trump withdrew the United States from the Paris Climate Accord, that in October 2018 the United Nations Intergovernmental Panel on Climate Change—not a panel known for exaggeration or rhetorical liberties—released something called the "doomsday report." This is what the executive director of the UN Environment Program, Erik Solheim, said about it: "It's like a deafening, piercing smoke alarm going off in the kitchen."

There is a smoke alarm in the kitchen, and there was smoke hovering over my place, my habitat. I don't know if the 1.8 degrees Fahrenheit the earth has warmed since the late 1800s caused those fires directly, or what kind of calamities might come of the 1.5 degrees it's predicted to warm by 2040. But irrespective of their cause, the fires' impact—the claustrophobia, the tension, the suffocating, ugly air—felt like a preview (and a mild one) of what's to come if we don't take immediate and drastic steps to halt and mitigate climate change. Temperatures will almost certainly rise. Air quality will almost certainly decline. I do not want to live like this, and you don't, either.

It's easy, if you are not in immediate danger of being swallowed by the sea or strangled by drought, to slip into normalcy. Moment to moment, for a lot of people in the United States and other wealthy nations, everything still feels fine, unchanged. Even if you genuinely believe that doom is coming, it is possible to set aside your panic for a while and, say, go get a coffee. Wash your dog. Bicker with your spouse. The stoplights still work and you can still buy avocados at the supermarket and life is still as mundane and tedious as it's always been. Boredom is somehow even more reassuring than happiness.

But we're well past the window of procrastination. This is the time.

Seattle in the smoke looks like one of those old photos of the United States' smog-socked skylines from before the Clean Air Act and the Environmental Protection Agency, an echo as oddly hopeful as it is horrifying. The thing about human-made climate change is that it's human made, which means that humans, to some degree, can unmake it. But it will take more than banning plastic bags and obsessing about straws and good liberals composting their pizza boxes.

We need to remember what a society is for.

Bad actors who profit from our despair, complacency, and delusions of rugged individualism have managed to convince us that we have no collective duty to prevent human beings from dying on the street today or in a generation or two due to not being able to breathe or find clean water. We must push ourselves beyond this cognitive divide, where some people see impending doom and shrug and others have the luxury to pretend they don't see it at all (come on, on some level, you have to see it); where everyone's house is a nation-state and life is a Hunger Game.

On tour for my 2016 book, *Shrill*, I was taking an Uber (I know, I'm sorry, it was a necessity*) across an unfamiliar town when the driver, whom I'll call Randy, started telling me about this cool dude named Jesus. Randy's big opener, earlier in the ride, had been to gesture at a homeless man panhandling by the side of the road and say, "Isn't it terrible?"

"Yeah," I agreed, though I was unsure whether he was referring to homelessness as a blight or as a form of state violence. "I can't believe my tax money pays for the president's golf vacations while people are freezing to death on the street. It's robbery."

"True that," he said, to my relief. "I hope this crazy country gets itself figured out before things get worse."

"Me, too," I said. "I would really like to keep living."

"Yeah?" Randy pounced. "How would you like to live . . . forever?"

Unfortunately, his offer had the opposite of its intended effect, as I immediately and permanently died. The undeterred Randy proceeded to explain to my corpse

---

* PSA: Ride share apps are so cheap because drivers are being exploited. If you have to use one, tip 30 percent minimum and in the meantime fight like hell for unionization and workers' rights. Bye!

that Christmas isn't real and the Bible predicted that the earth was round, which was proof that the Bible was scientific fact. This went on for the next twenty minutes, during which Randy got lost twice as he was apparently proselytizing too hard to look at the GPS. It was less a ride share and more a low-grade kidnapping for which I was being charged. To his credit, though, it did feel like eternity.

But if there's anything twenty-first-century American life has prepared me for, it's an old man taking possession of my body and incompetently steering it in directions I don't want to go, while ignoring my boundaries and lecturing me on the one right way to live. At least Randy cared about that homeless guy, though. And that is more than I can say for leadership in America.

I've been thinking a lot lately about the notion of "care." Care can be florid and romantic or bureaucratic and dry; it is maintenance and stewardship and only sometimes love. You can take care of something without personally caring about it, which is precisely what our elected officials are supposed to do: take care of our communities and our planet, whether or not they personally share our priorities and fears and weaknesses and religions and sexual orientations and gender identities and skin colors.

But in this moment, at precisely the moment when it is already too late for our planet in many ways but in which we could still do something, if anyone cared, the United

States is being run by a political party that is thoroughly divested of care. Since Trump took office, Republicans have proposed legislation to destroy unions, the health care system, the education system, and the Environmental Protection Agency; to defund Planned Parenthood and obliterate abortion access; to stifle public protest and decimate arts funding; to increase the risk of violence against trans people and roll back antidiscrimination laws; and to funnel more and more wealth from the poorest to the richest.

In the wake of the Republican Party's luscious, succulent failure to obliterate the Affordable Care Act in 2017 and replace it with catastrophic nationwide poverty and death, an old video of a Paul Ryan gaffe went viral. "We're not going to give up," Ryan assured his audience, "on destroying the health care system for the American people."

The clip is from 2013, not 2017, and obviously Ryan did not mean to say into a microphone that he wanted to destroy the health care system. He also, presumably, did not mean to let Donald Trump spell the end of his political career so he could retire to spend more time with his teenage children—just around the time all kids are known to want their dads to spend less time taking health care from poor people and more time just hanging out.

But here's the thing: I talk into a microphone in front of people all the time, and not once have I ever accidentally said, "Hitler was pretty cool" when what I meant to say was "Throw all Nazis off a bridge." Even if we acknowledge that such a slip of the tongue is technically possible (if not likely), we don't need to wonder about what Ryan secretly believes. Gaffe or no, we already know he wants to destroy the health care system for the American people, because he tried to pass legislation that would destroy the health care system for the American people. Stop doubting what you see right in front of your face. Climate change is real. Criminalizing homelessness does not stop homelessness. Universal health care is an objective public good. Corporations are stealing your money and your future.

Political parties do tell you what they are and what they think a society is for, maybe not in their words but always, always, always in their actions. But politicians don't actually get to decide what their duties and responsibilities are and what view of the world they're tasked to uphold—we do. And I don't think it's a particularly wild swing for me to say that the purpose of a society is *not* to generate the maximum amount of megabucks for oil and gas executives and pharmaceutical executives and auto executives and defense contractors and corrupt old men moldering in the halls of Congress. The purpose of a society is to take care of people. FIRE. EVERY. DIRTY. MOTHERFUCKER. WHO DOESN'T CARE IF YOUR GRANDBABY DIES IN A FLASH FLOOD IN DOWNTOWN TUCSON. MY GOD.

The other day I accidentally read a Facebook post about climate change during Aham's and my sacred morning time—a post that said, basically, "It's over." We missed the window. Climate collapse is imminent and inevitable, and our brains cannot truly comprehend what "exponential" looks like, because right now everything looks relatively normal in the privileged parts of the world—the other day I saw orca whales, through binoculars, *from inside my mother's living room*—but it also looks like death. Soon. Everything will change drastically and abruptly, we will burn and the sea will swallow us, even the rich, and my generation is not going to die before it gets here. Fuck dreams. Fuck sending your kids to college. Fuck fun. Fuck art. Fuck fish. It isn't the next generation's job to fix climate change; that was our job, and we didn't even try. All our kids can do is learn to farm and hope they survive mass extinction.

I rolled over and clutched Aham as tight as I could and sobbed into his back in absolute true fucking grieving terror. (I ruined the morning.) We were a few days into Donald Trump's fake national emergency to build his racist propaganda wall; meanwhile, a real emergency, the most catastrophic global emergency in the history of the human race, was entering its last days and the most powerful man on Earth was insisting that the gravest threat to American safety is refugee children. And for what? For fucking what? I don't get to die of old age holding hands with my husband so that a couple of billionaires can accumulate $111 billion instead of $109 billion to pass on to their probably dead children in an apocalyptic wasteland where twenty-first-century currency is worthless anyway because it's really more of a scrap-metal-and-goat-lard-based economy? No wonder there's an opioid epidemic.

During the 2019 State of the Union address, Trump bragged, "We have unleashed a revolution in American energy—the United States is now the number one producer of oil and natural gas in the world."

A week or so later, on Twitter, Trump mocked Amy Klobuchar for "talking proudly of fighting global warming while standing in a virtual blizzard of snow, ice and freezing temperatures. Bad timing. By the end of her speech she looked like a Snowman(woman)!"

He's laughing at you. He's laughing at your land drying up and your children starving to death. But just as we have begun to tell men like this that they do not own and control our bodies, we do not have to let them own and control our future on this planet.

My fellow human beings. Wherever you live. Whomever you voted for. You know those things that mean everything to you—your exquisite loves—whatever your version is, your evergreen trees, your mornings, your cold waters, your Dad-haunted hills, your Ahamefule? Human-made climate change is going to take those things from you and kill them. We will not get to die in the normal ways, quietly, comfortably, together, at home, old. We will die in pain and panic. Or your grandchildren will. They will be panicked and in pain and will never have seen snow on the mountains in the summertime, as you and I got to.

Do you understand? Even if the notion of this happening in your lifetime or the lifetime of people you love is only a possibility, a prognostication, don't you want to fight it with every atom in your body? Build it into your day. Every day you call. Every day you write a letter. Every march you march. Tax yourself. Protect your community. If you're waiting for a grown-up to come fix it, stop. Be your own grown-up. Be your own president.

I know that people you trust told you that climate disaster isn't real, but they were lying, because they know that's what you want to hear, because they are corrupt and they want power and money. That's it. Luckily, we are their boss. They are hired to take care of us, and if they are lighting the candles and setting the table for fire and death, we have to get rid of them and give the power to someone who will fight for this world, because—and I think this goes cruelly underacknowledged in the surreal, nihilistic upside down of Trump's America—this world is beautiful and good and worth saving. Do not despair. Despair is the death of action. Go, act, fight.

After my sobbing, I spent the rest of the day talking myself down. That post I read was just one man's analysis of the data; other scientists have other takes; we do not actually know what will happen when, though I believe it is dire and soon. Regardless, we cannot go back in time; all we can do is start right now. We do not actually have to convince and mobilize seven billion people; we just have to convince and mobilize our governments. Donald Trump is the president of only one country; there are 195 countries on Earth. Regulation works; people, for the most part, will live within the parameters presented to them. We don't know what we don't know; we don't know what technologies the will to live might wring out of the best of us.

I love this world, and I aim to keep it.

Long Live the Port Chester Whooping Cranes

I was parallel parking between two Priuses when my stepdaughter, who is fifteen, asked, "Lindy, why do people hate Priuses so much?"

"Do they?" I didn't know that. I thought Priuses were cool. Tom Hanks drives one. I mean, *I* hate Priuses because their rear seat belts aren't long enough for fat people, so I have to risk my life in one bonus way every time I get into a Lyft (you too, Tesla, but thank God you reinvented the door handle—it's about time!), which seems to me like a passive-aggressive side effect of wellness culture: energy-efficient cars are for smart, conscientious, energy-efficient people. If fat people don't want their brains pulverized on the hot gravel shoulder of I-5, they should eat less and exercise more!

But the general public hates Priuses? Really? Do they hate noted Prius owner *Cameron Diaz*, too??

"Yeah, the kids at my school make fun of Priuses all the time."

Oh, right, I remembered, a whiff of familiarity drifting up from my youth. Because caring about the environment is—as they said in the nineties—gay.

My younger stepdaughter goes to an exurban high school about an hour outside of Seattle, near her mom's house. It's a mostly white school (over 75 percent) and significantly more conservative than any community within the city limits. The county went for Hillary but had almost twice as many votes for Trump as King County, where I live. More than a few kids wear MAGA hats to school, partially because they, like their parents, sincerely think that Trump is good and his ideas are good and his policies rule and immigrants are bad and liberals are snowflakes. But there's a subtler, more ironic cast to it, too: wearing a MAGA hat is a form of trolling, to "trigger" the libs and the feminists, because if there's one legacy Trump is leaving to children (besides an irreparably ravaged ecosystem, a nation stripped of civil rights protections, and maybe another war), it's the gamification of harm.

My older stepdaughter, who's seventeen, went to that school for her freshman year before transferring to an inner-city school near our house. "My science teacher there told us that he doesn't believe in the Big Bang," she said when I asked about the science curriculum at her old school, her sister's school. In her art class, a kid drew a fetus's hand reaching for a woman's hand, with a pair of scissors labeled "ABORTION" slicing between them. Her city school doesn't always have potable water. Her exurb school had a laptop for every student. She doesn't miss it.

Of course the kids of Trump supporters think that Priuses—which, by the way, are still mass transit–killing, fossil fuel–burning luxury items manufactured by the automotive industry, so, yes, extremely granola—are effeminate and embarrassing, virtue signaling for cucks, because waste is manly and destruction is manly and real manly men drive trucks guns bang bang toot toot truck deer beer mud truck vroom black smoke logging antlers tits fire and blood.

I started to explain: "So, okay, in the year 2000, a man named Al Gore ran for president, and he cared about the environment, and he lost, kind of, and after that . . . people thought . . . Democrats . . . drank lattes? And drove Volvos, which was, um, stuck up, I think. And this is like an extension of that, I guess." She was already back on her phone.

But no. That's not right. You have to go way, way back. Barbara Ehrenreich summed it up efficiently in the *New York Times* in 2004, in a column about Michael Moore. She described how the notion of a liberal elite had started on the left, among anarchists and Trotskyites in the early twentieth century who had "noted, correctly, that the Soviet Union was spawning a 'new class' of power-mad bureaucrats." Many of those thinkers had "mutated into neocons in the 60's," and they had taken the theory with them—an invaluable contribution to the American Right.

"Backed up by the concept of a 'liberal elite,' right-wingers could crony around with their corporate patrons in luxuriously appointed think tanks and boardrooms—all the while purporting to represent the average overworked Joe," she wrote. "Beyond that, the idea of a liberal elite nourishes the right's perpetual delusion that it is a tiny band of patriots bravely battling an evil power structure."

The right-wing Club for Growth calling Howard Dean a "tax-hiking, government-expanding, latte-drinking, sushi-eating, Volvo-driving, *New York Times*–reading, body-piercing, Hollywood-loving, left-wing freak show" in a 2003 attack ad was just one data point in a decades-long propaganda campaign to cast the American Left as the real enemy of the "real" people. But it was much darker than that, even worse than giving right-wingers a smoke screen to appeal to the working class or stroking their underdog fetish. The myth of the "liberal elite" strategically frames liberal values—environmentalism, racial and gender equality, gay and trans liberation, immigrants' rights, the social safety net—as inherently frivolous, dishonest, a joke. By extension, the people who would benefit from the actualization of those values are "fake" Americans—the nation's most vulnerable groups being called decadent effetes by the most feckless, corrupt, undeserving legacy hires history has ever seen, people who have all the advantages in the world and still need to buy their kids' way into college.

By 2019, the far Right's unflagging message that it alone is the steward of "real" America—and Democrats are the party of venality, of snobbery, of self-interest cynically masked as beneficence—has come to full fruition, its ultimate purpose revealed: to justify the stigmatization of care itself.

It's not just caring about the environment that's effeminate and therefore despicable, it's caring about anything. It's *care.*

If you train people to scoff at community and stewardship—at tending to the needs of others, yes, but also at advocating for oneself—you can do whatever you want to them and they will not complain. You can strip away their ability to earn a living wage, to send their kids to college, to retire. You can undermine their most sacred values. You can allow children to be massacred, and they'll weep for the guns.

This is toxic masculinity at its most pitiful. How sad—and I don't mean that with disgust, it is truly, profoundly *sad*—to let us all die because you've been taught that wanting not to die is cowardice; that vulnerability is weakness; that anything short of charging into the increasingly brief future, assault rifle blazing, exhaust belching, with half-chewed feedlot steak falling out of your mouth, constitutes some sort of romantic tongue kiss with a perfect male figure skater, *and that a romantic tongue kiss with a perfect male figure skater would be something worth genociding the planet to avoid.*

How did we let it get this bad?

I remember sitting in physics class on the first day of the World Trade Organization protests in Seattle in 1999. I was a senior, still seventeen, and we'd been hearing for weeks that a HUGE and BAD anarchist riot was coming to destroy the town, with bombs and cops and garbage fires and tanks and bricks and marching bands and naked bicyclists with their choo-choos out and people dressed as turtles. *Turtles!* The Gap was on high alert!

My understanding, at the time, was that activist types—"hippies" we called them in the nineties, a semiderisive and semi-ironic catchall for people who cared about stuff enough to make signs—were mad about globalization, which, as I understood it at the time, was something to do with money, which I assumed was morally neutral (INCORRECT), sweatshop labor, which I recognized as bad, and the killing of sea turtles, very bad. Inasmuch as I could formulate an opinion on something that I did not understand whatsoever, I was on the side of the hippies, even the Gap smashers probably. I was certainly not on the side of the cops. At least I knew that much.

But I remember, on that day, a procession of protestors (almost certainly, if I had to guess, from the alternative school across the street) barreling down the hall outside my physics class, yelling and waving signs and banging drums, trying to entice other kids to march downtown with them and join the throng of 40,000. My classmates and I looked at one another, the call of the wild tugging at us just a bit, the yearning to be one of those kids who isn't scared of sincerity, of action, of authority (my mother had forbidden me to go within a mile of the protests), to go out and do something just because it mattered. To be the kind of smart, engaged young person who actually understood things about *the globe.*

Only one kid out of thirty grabbed his bag and walked out.

I just remember feeling, with innate certainty, that *he was a different kind of person from me.*

In the 1990s, activism—particularly student activism—was stigmatized as tedious, silly, self-important to the point of narcissism, and, most damningly, ineffectual. Student activism was Paul Rudd smirking behind designer sunglasses in the 1995 movie *Clueless*: "I'm going to a Tree People meeting. We're trying to get Marky Mark to plant a celebrity tree."

It was Alicia Silverstone in *Clueless*, too, trying on activism for a day to impress a boy:

"I'm captain of the Pismo Beach Disaster Relief!"

"I don't think they need your skis."

"Daddy, some people lost all their belongings. Don't you think that includes athletic equipment?"

If you were very, very cool in the early to midnineties, you could pull off a Beastie Boys "Free Tibet" bumper sticker or quote Rage Against the Machine in your social studies paper, but for your middle-of-the-road fat white dorks? The safest path, if you were both uncool and had no backbone, was to say all the right things about freedom and equality while rolling your eyes at the try-hards.

I want to be very clear that I'm not talking about kids of marginalized identities, communities who have never for one second had the luxury to choose whether to fight or not. I'm talking about the average white kids, the comfortable kids, the suburban kids, who were too insecure or too self-involved to care about anything, who let *Saved by the Bell* soothe their little consciences to sleep because wasn't Jessie Spano fucking annoying? Those kids grew up to be the great, white, complacent center—the nonvoters, the apolitical, the ones who just stay out of it, as though inaction isn't a political stance.

There was always reverence for "real" activists, of course—the civil rights movement, the suffragettes, Cesar Chavez, Harvey Milk—people who had lived and died and won great battles before we were born. But social justice activism as a continuum, a mantle to take up, a garden to tend and defend, a *moral obligation* (particularly for those of us born into comfort and power) was harder to see. Contemporary activists were human hacky-sacks with suspect motives or imperfect methods or fleeting loyalties or any other number of manufactured excuses as to why they weren't legitimate, weren't *the same* as our parents marching to end segregation on the same streets a couple decades before.

This artificial divide between past and present is a tactic I recognize now among certain sects of antifeminism and the alt-right, the ones still shy of overt Nazism, still striving for plausible deniability. Second-wave feminists were legitimate feminists, men used to tweet at me between flurries of harassment, believing that the concession worked as a kind of camouflage. *Of course* women should have the vote, checking accounts, birth control, jobs. It's the third- and fourth-wave feminists they have a problem with—the "identitarians," the "professional victims"—who demand equality not just in politics (as though we have that) but in culture. The ones for whom it isn't enough for rape to be illegal but who want society to examine the behaviors that foster and enable sexual predation in the first place. The ones who want to have recreational sex but don't want to be raped. The ones who are all about "safe, legal" abortion but reject the compulsory "rare."

The modern right loves to quote Dr. Martin Luther King, Jr., a "real" activist, while deriding Black Lives Matter. They claim to support social justice in the abstract but hate "social justice warriors." They're all for freedom and equality, they say, but sneer at the mechanisms that might actually help get us there—affirmative action, deplatforming Nazis, reparations, voting rights for felons, prison abolition, respectful adjustments to language—as bleeding-heart pandering to the dreaded "political correctness."

In the 1994 comedy *PCU*, a preppy high school kid goes to visit a prospective college, the fictional Port Chester University, and falls under the guidance of a hundredth-year senior played by Jeremy Piven. "It's a whole new ball game on campus these days," Piven tells him, "and they call it PC. Politically Correct. And it's not just politics, it's everything—it's what you eat, it's what you wear, and it's what you say. If you don't watch yourself, you'll get in a buttload of trouble." The kid, being a classic, all-American boy-guy just trying to have a cool time, does get into a buttload of trouble, because all you have to do to get in trouble with those oversensitive PC types is *nothing*.

At PCU, the Greek system has been disbanded and the student body has splintered into various political factions: the potheads, the radical feminists ("Those aren't women, Tom, those are womynists"), the angry and paranoid Afrocentrics, the dirtbag white boys (our heroes, of fucking course), the Young Republicans, the dilettante causeheads ("They find a world-threatening issue and stick with it for about a week"), and so on. Walking across the quad, prefrosh and Piven encounter a litany of obviously very stupid causes: "Save the whales!" "Gays in the military now!" "Free Nelson Mandela!" "They freed him already." "Oh."

Meanwhile, the bad-mommy principal is trying to change the mascot from "the offensive Port Chester Indian" to the endangered whooping crane. Can you imagine?? What a horrible PC bitch! In the end, she is fired, definitely with cause!

Early in the film, Piven and the kid have a close encounter with the womynists, one of whom turns out to be Piven's ex. The other womynists are not happy, because they are militant and only want to stomp phalluses!

"You went out with a white male?"

"I was a freshman!"

"Freshperson, please."

That was what a feminist looked like, to anyone who didn't actually know any feminists, in 1994.

Do I think the screenwriters of *PCU* genuinely didn't think that Nelson Mandela should be free? Or that they yearned for the eradication of whales? Of course not. It's a comedy. But the joke of the movie was to paint student activism—which, sure, can occasionally be overzealous and underbaked just like any other youthful pursuit—as a farce, the opposite of fun. It's a deterrent. It's not a coincidence that, in 2014, Tucker Carlson's propaganda shitrag The Daily Caller would call *PCU* "the best-known unknown movie in America with a Nostradamian capability of predicting what would happen to higher education—and the country as a whole—20 years after its release."

The term *political correctness* (much like the slimy *pro-life*) is a right-wing neologism, a tactical bending of reality, an attempt to colonize the playing field, a bluff to lure dupes into dignifying propaganda. True to form, the credulous Left adopted it wholesale in the early nineties—*PCU* was very much of the zeitgeist—electively embroiling us in three decades of bad-faith "debate" over whether discouraging white people from using racial slurs constitutes government censorship. Of course it doesn't. Debate over. Treating anti-PC arguments as anything but a bad-faith distraction props up the lie that it is somehow unfair to identify and point out racism, let alone fight to eradicate it. Pointing out and fighting to eradicate racism is how we build the racism-free world that all but racists profess to want.

Today, the anti-PC set frames political correctness as a sovereign entity, separate from real human beings—like an advisory board or a nutritional label or a silly after-school club that one can heed or ignore with no moral implications—as though if we simply reject political correctness we can keep, say, the Washington Redskins without harming native communities. But the reality is that there's no such thing as political correctness; it's a rhetorical device to depersonalize oppression.

Being cognizant of and careful with the historic trauma of others is what "political correctness" means. It means that the powerful should never attack the disempowered—

not because it "offends" them or hurts their "feelings" but because it perpetuates toxic, oppressive systems. Or, in plainer language, because it makes people's lives worse. In tangible ways. For generations.

I don't know, call me a total causehead, but I kind of feel like it's progress that we live in a world where dumping raw meat on a peaceful vegan protest and "[installing] speed bumps on the handicapped ramps" (real *PCU* plot points!) are no longer considered good jokes. Just my 1.636 cents (to a man's two)!

If you were a privileged white kid in the nineties who could feel a moral pull to fight for something but didn't know where to start, looking to the media for inspiration was a dry, dry well. We had the joyless ecofeminists Lisa Simpson and Darlene from *Roseanne*. We had *South Park*'s Wendy Testaburger, who spent a significant bulk of her screen time being vomited on by Stan. Kat from *10 Things I Hate About You* is a rabid feminist until she's cured by getting a boyfriend. Topanga's feminism on *Boy Meets World* was often a punch line (in her vision of a utopian future, Topanga says, "we moved all men underground and use them just for breeding"). Again, on *Saved by the Bell*, a show for children, Jessie was relentlessly mocked for calling out Slater's chauvinism. It was a running gag for the entire series.

The feminist cultural critic Anita Sarkeesian, in her video series *Tropes vs. Women*, calls these Straw Feminists:

> The Straw Feminist character is part of a fictional post-feminist world that only exists in Hollywood, the trope is a tool that's used to promote the fallacy that everyone is already equal.
>
> What's exceptionally frustrating is that these characters often bring up legitimate feminist concerns about women's rights and women's equality but those concerns are quickly undermined by the writers making the characters seem over the top, crazy, and extremist.

Care, but just a little. A cool amount. This was the status quo protecting itself.

I should say here that I am oversimplifying things. I didn't go to the WTO protests when I was seventeen, but I did take action, a little, on the things that I could understand. One time in elementary school, I wrote a letter to the mayor suggesting that he build a train that could take people all over the city. He was like "Thanks!" Most people don't know that it was my idea, but Seattle's Link Light Rail is estimated to be finished in 2041. You're welcome! In eighth grade I danced in a dance-a-thon fund-raiser for a nonprofit that provided nutritious meals to people living with HIV, and in high school I bowled in a bowl-a-thon fund-raiser for something I forget, while dressed as Abraham Lincoln.

I took part in a program at my high school that trained students to facilitate classroom discussions about prejudice. We went on a retreat, we did bonding exercises, kids smoked in the woods, and we came back to our deeply segregated school (a by-product of a poorly implemented gifted program in a systemically racist city) in a historically redlined neighborhood and spent one class period talking about racism, awkwardly. Twenty years later, that historically black neighborhood is almost entirely gentrified—the *Seattle Times* estimates that by 2025 it could be less than 10 percent black. Some of my white classmates own houses there now.

The directive transmitted by *PCU* and the Straw Feminists to the comfortable class wasn't never to care; it was to avoid caring too much. It's the perfect cover, really.

I did not go to the WTO protest partially because my mom told me I couldn't and partially because I didn't understand it but primarily because I'd been taught that when ordinary people try to do activism, they look stupid. Of course now I know that there is no effective activism without the passion and commitment of ordinary people and it is a basic duty of the privileged to show up and fight for issues that don't affect us directly. But maintaining that separation has served the status quo well. It keeps good people always just shy of taking action. It's tone policing. It's the white moderate. But it's changing.

One recent afternoon, my older daughter paused while passing through the living room with a carton of mealworms to feed to her leopard gecko (my beautiful granddaughter, Richard Pepperoni B. Jordan), and asked, "Are you guys busy tomorrow night?"

"Probably," my husband said. "Why?"

"Oh, you know how I'm in the Art of Resistance and Resilience Club? We're finally unveiling our Black Panthers mural. Bobby Seale is going to be there, and I'm giving a speech. Well, actually, it's more of a poem. You guys can come if you want to." Shrug, bye.

First of all, no, we did not know that she was in the Art of Resistance and Resilience Club. We did not know that, somehow, in between Mock Trial and student government and the spring musical and Feminist Union and *regular* Art Club she had also been painting a mural honoring the Black Panther Party for the past six months. We did not know that she gave speeches or wrote poems or that she was acquainted with Bobby Seale, who founded the Black Panther Party with Huey P. Newton in Oakland in 1966. But okay, you radiant freak! Do you have a secret second family, too, and you sneak out Tuesdays and Thursdays to be their daughter? Are you also the CEO of the Cheesecake Factory?

We canceled our plans.

The mural is spectacular, at the intersection of the two major arterials that carry drivers from fully gentrified central Seattle to quickly gentrifying south Seattle. Images of Black Panthers distributing food and registering black voters stretch forty feet along the sidewalk outside the high school, which is 93 percent kids of color. Portraits of Seattle Black Panther Party members stand defiant among pamphlets about COINTELPRO and swaths of West African wax prints. I asked her if they had treated the paint somehow to make it easier to remove graffiti. "No one would tag this mural," she said. At the time of this writing, no one has.

I asked her what, if anything, they had been taught about the Black Panther Party at her old school, also a public school, only forty-five minutes away. "That they were terrorists," she said.

The world feels really bad right now. If anything, obviously, attending a Bobby Seale teach-in at an underfunded public school in a city that is minting overnight millionaires should be a reminder that, for many people in this country, that "bad" feeling has been normal for a very long time. Donald Trump may be singularly jarring in his recreational cruelty and callous incompetence, but there has never been an America that is safe and just for black people. Ever. Trump was a foregone conclusion, an inevitable effluvient of the systemic rot in the deepest heart of the American experiment. Yes, his America is terrifying, but only the most privileged could claim that things were fine before or that a return to the "normal" of November 7, 2016, would be anything approaching justice. The problem with America is that we refuse to look at the problem with America.

Still, though, there is something about this moment—perhaps it's David Attenborough finally hammering the reality of climate catastrophe into our lazy, avoidant little brains—that inspires a particular hopelessness, a contagious, nihilistic fatigue. Shit just feels *weird* right now. But standing in a high school cafeteria watching a hundred teenagers raptly raising black power fists, all sincerity, all determination, while eighty-two-year-old Bobby Seale calls them to remember the past, reminds them that others know the secrets of how to fight this battle because this battle is as old as this nation—that's hope.

Activism comes so naturally to my girls. They are native to it. They are not afraid of sincerity. They're at every protest, ones I haven't even heard about. Sure, there's a concomitant swell among young people on the right, of conservative kids encouraged by Trumpism to keep their parents' prejudices fresh, to memeify cruelty, roast Priuses, and own the libs with their hats. But this generation wasn't fed activism as a punch line the way I was, and as Trump emboldens conservative teenagers, my daughters and their friends aren't cowed—they're galvanized.

Think of sixteen-year-old Greta Thunberg, whose stone-faced protest outside the Swedish Parliament in 2018 inspired student strikes in more than a dozen countries and made her a global voice on climate change. Thunberg, addressing the United Nations when she was just fifteen, told world leaders that they were "behaving like children" and said, "For 25 years countless people have come to the UN climate conferences begging our world leaders to stop emissions and clearly that has not worked as emissions are continuing to rise. So I will not beg the world leaders to care for our future. I will instead let them know change is coming whether they like it or not."

Think of the Parkland mass shooting survivors, who, in the thick of unimaginable trauma, rejected the typical thoughts, prayers, and shrugs from their government—the blatant lie that there simply is no way to keep children from being slaughtered at school—and helped pass sixty-seven new gun laws in 2018.

Those kids were born after 9/11 into a fractured place. They didn't get any quiet years, I guess, when, in many communities (not all, of course) the end of the world felt abstract and far away. Young people are here and strong and smart and fierce, and they do not intend to die. They are artists and scientists and leaders, and we just have to show up and fight for them, and with them, every day until we die. It is not their job to save us—we are the parents—but may they inspire us to help them save themselves. I feel afraid in this moment, but I do not feel hopeless.

In the auditorium, my stepdaughter takes the mic.

"They are scared when we march, they are scared when we sit," she chants with disgust as her poem builds to its conclusion. "They are scared of the fact that we are tired of their shit. We are tired of the fact that we still have to fight for what the white man gets to call his inalienable rights. And it's not how we fight, it's that we dare to." She takes a deep breath. "So we, as a people, will keep fighting, whether it's peaceful or scary, until we reach justice by whatever means necessary."

Tomorrow Is the First Day

The INS Building—formerly the US Immigration Station & Assay Office—processed all immigrants arriving in and departing from Seattle from 1932 to 2004 and has since been converted into low-cost artist studios. I have a little corner room there, which I inherited from a musician friend and share with another writer. A placard outside the wing where my office is located reads, "SOLITARY CONFINEMENT: The three isolation cells that occupied this corner of the detention dorm were original to the building. INS would isolate detainees who were disruptive in here, though they were often people with mental health issues."

My mother, who still lives by a pregentrification (pre-Amazon-dot-com) mental map of which parts of Seattle are "seedy" and which ones are "safe," often warns me not to walk to the train too late. The neighborhood, once a desolate industrial triangle nestled between Chinatown and the football stadium, is now bustling with tech workers and food trucks, though casualties of Seattle's homeless epidemic still beg for help from the alleys. She needn't worry either way. The building is a haunted place, haunted enough in broad daylight, too haunted to work till midnight.

My mom remembers her older brothers and sisters going to the INS Building with their dad maybe once a year, until they became naturalized citizens at eighteen. She was the sixth child of seven, the first born in the United States after her parents moved to Seattle from Norway in the late 1940s. She didn't understand why her siblings got to go down to the INS Building and she didn't, but it seemed special, a ritual they got to do with Dad. She felt jealous.

My extended family is beamingly, fawningly proud of our immigrant story: My great grandparents moved from Norway to North Dakota thanks to the Homestead Act, which offered "free," "unoccupied" acreage to settlers willing to cultivate it, forcing native tribes off their ancestral lands to make way for huge waves of white immigration. When the Great Depression hit, my grandmother, then eighteen years old and the eldest of ten, was sent back to Norway with two of her little sisters to ease the burden on the family. There she married my grandfather, and the two eventually emigrated to Seattle. Those are the three branches of my family: Seattle, North Dakota, and Norway.

Some of my conservative family members occasionally post about politics on Facebook, as most of us do. I've seen anti-immigration screeds from these proud children of immigrants, regurgitating Trumpisms about dangerous migrants taking over "our" country. I've seen relatives decry the Standing Rock water protectors from their homes on land stolen and given to us—not an abstract "us," as in white colonial settlers and their descendants, but *literally us*, literally our family.

In my office, where "disruptive" human beings were once imprisoned because they violated the Chinese Exclusion Act by seeking a new life on their own terms, I procrastinate by checking the news. In 2019, that meant reading *a lot* about Trump's sadistic, symbolic border wall; Trump calling the mayor of London a "loser"; Trump not seeming to care that the country in his charge averages one mass shooting a day.

Maybe that's the news today. Does it have to be the news tomorrow?

Diet culture is a coercive, misogynist pyramid scheme that saps women's economic and political power, but there is one tenet I still hang on to: Every day is new. Broke your diet and ate a Snickers* today? Fine. Tomorrow is the day

* GOOD FOR YOU! THOSE ARE GOOD! IT IS OKAY TO FEEL PLEASURE!

you start. You fail again, you start again. No matter how many times you fail, you can still start. Don't let today swallow tomorrow.

I recently rewatched the 1978 Hal Ashby film *Coming Home*, starring Jane Fonda as a bored officer's wife during the Vietnam War and Jon Voight as the sweet, angry, paraplegic veteran who captivates her—both in Oscar-winning turns. To pass the time, Fonda volunteers at a hospital for wounded veterans—a hospital for kids coming back in pieces, too poor to afford private care—and she's shocked by what she finds: short supplies, shorter staff, poor sanitation, blood and urine on the floor, traumatized young men with nowhere to go. She runs to the other officers' wives to tell them what she's seen—*we have to do something!* They brush her off. That's not really their *thing*. They don't want to get their hands dirty.

That moment knocked me over, that moment in 1968, when the film takes place, when those veterans were still boys, when we, as a society, could have caught them and we didn't. Americans love to overwrite their own memory—to remake cruelty as clumsiness, victims as perpetrators—but this wasn't an accident. We knew we were failing them even then, and we let it happen. We chose it.

And we knew we were failing them still, ten years later, when Fonda and Ashby made *Coming Home*, and we could have started then, begun shoring up the damage done by the previous decade of inaction. We didn't.

Coming Home is fictional, obviously, but those kids in the hospital existed in real life in hospitals all over the country. They're old men now, and a good number of Vietnam veterans are currently without housing on the streets of San Francisco, Portland, New York, and Seattle, my city, a city absolutely thick with millionaires thanks to Washington state's outrageous lack of an income tax. We, and they, couldn't even have fathomed how hard we were going to fail them.

There is always a day, crystalline, tantalizing, diminishing behind us, that was just before the point of no return. When we knew, but we didn't act. If only we could go back. Well, today is that day. Tomorrow is that day.

Tomorrow is that day if we start telling the right stories, start living in the truth, and holding the line even when it hurts—if the art we create reinforces the idea that we have the power to change all this if we choose, and that all people have the right to decide what happens tomorrow.

After Trump was elected, when people found out that I write political columns for a living, they'd often say something like "Trump must be great for business! Plenty to write about!" Um, yeah, it's great. I love it. In this moment, it seems as though there is more noise than ever before in my lifetime—more atrocities per minute, more scandals per second. It can feel difficult to know what to say. Because if there's one perversely welcome side effect of the Trump era, it's that everything is on the table.

I used to think of my job as digesting the news, digesting the chatter, then saying what still needed to be said—whatever hard truths people were avoiding or invisible biases they were overlooking. What is different now—in this moment, as we try to decide where to go after Trump and how much we are still willing to let them do—is that we have finally managed to name so many problems that were so long in shadow. We know that lax gun laws turn male rage into massacres. We know that we have about ten years to mitigate irreversible, catastrophic climate disaster. There is no longer any pretense among the intellectually honest that the people who have enabled this president's rise to power are anything but a white supremacist organized crime network and its willing dupes. It's increasingly clear that borders are ghoulish.

As the 2020 campaign kicks into gear already—sooner than I am ready for yet not soon enough—I have been thinking of 2016, of the time before.

In the last days of that campaign, my husband said to me, "This election is part of the Civil War." On Trump's inauguration day, my friend Tracy Rector, an Indigenous activist and filmmaker, wrote on Facebook, "The slave masters have taken control." Those who believe that straight white men have a mandate to burn the rest of us as fuel, to sell us for parts, to mow us down and climb up the pile, never truly conceded that war. They have been biding their time, and this is their last great gambit. But I live in the America that won—the America with art and empathy and a free press and fierce protest to dig out the rot. The truth is our power and our craft.

We've won this war before, and we will win it again.

Tomorrow can be the first day.

The witches are coming, but not for your life. We're coming for your lies. We're coming for your legacy. We're coming for our future

Acknowledgments

This book would not exist without the brilliance and unflagging support of Rachel Dry, Gary Morris, Samantha Irby, Amelia Bonow, Guy Branum, Angela Garbes, Lauren Hoffman, Martha Plimpton, Mary Ann Naples, Mauro DiPreta, Michelle Aielli, Jason Richman, Krishan Trotman, the *Shrill* TV team, the Hachette Books team, all my precious bros, Musashi's, Dough Zone, Canton Wonton House, Vientiane Asian Grocery, Beard Papa, SweeTarts, Dill Pickle Spitz, Coke Zero, Diet Coke, Coca-Cola Classic, coffee, water, milk, whipped cream, and my dear family: mom, dad, Charley, Penelope, Ijeoma, Jacque, Basil, Susan, and Ahamefule J. Oluo most of all. Words are inadequate to express my thanks. Not a single all-nighter was pulled during the writing of this book, and for that I thank myself. Maybe people really can change.